MAXIMIZE YOUR LIFE

MAXIMIZE YOUR LIFE

An Action Plan for the Indian Middle Class

Pavan K. Varma
&
Renuka Khandekar

PENGUIN
VIKING
An imprint of Penguin Random House

VIKING

USA | Canada | UK | Ireland | Australia
New Zealand | India | South Africa | China | Singapore

Viking is part of the Penguin Random House group of companies
whose addresses can be found at global.penguinrandomhouse.com

Published by Penguin Random House India Pvt. Ltd
4th Floor, Capital Tower 1, MG Road,
Gurugram 122 002, Haryana, India

Penguin
Random House
India

First published in Viking by Penguin Books India 2000

10 9 8 7 6 5 4 3 2

ISBN 9780670888948

Typeset in *New Brunswick* by SÜRYA, New Delhi
Printed at Replika Press Pvt. Ltd, India

www.penguin.co.in

I am having my share of trials and tests. I am not entitled to any pity, for it is all of my own making.

—Rajaji,
Private letter, 17 August 1953

Contents

Preface

This book is not a sequel to *The Great Indian Middle Class*, but it is certainly a consequence. Ever since *The Great Indian Middle Class* was published in April 1998, I have been speaking in innumerable forums on the need for educated Indians to show a sense of greater concern for the fact that India has the largest number of the abjectly poor on earth, and the largest concentration of people unable to read and write. India also has more people dying of malaria and tuberculosis and diarrhoea than anywhere else in the world. I made the point that it is our own self-interest that should impel us to try and change this situation, because we cannot insulate our lives, and the security and prosperity that we seek for ourselves and our children, from this ocean of deprivation and poverty.

For me it was quite a revelation to note that in

the question-answer sessions that followed, many, if not most, of the questions were indicative of a sense of helplessness about what an individual middle-class citizen could do. Many people said that they would like to do something more with their lives than merely a blind and obsessive pursuit of their own material well being at any cost, but did not know where to begin, whom to approach, what to do and how to reorganize the priorities of their lives. They were also besieged by self doubt: Would their contribution be of any value? What can an individual do? Is the whole exercise worth it?

Renuka Khandekar came up with a revelation of her own. She was then editing a women's magazine called *Zena*. Based on the analysis of *The Great Indian Middle Class*, she devoted one issue to enumerating the many things that ordinary middle-class Indians *could do*, in their own small way, that would make a visible difference to their own lives and to the quality of life around them. Renuka was overwhelmed by the response to this issue.

It was this which brought both of us together to work on a 'manual' that could hope to provide for many middle-class Indians the rationale and the tools for evolving into citizens rather than merely being passive residents of their town and city.

The premise of this book is that while India may be the world's largest democracy, with every passing day it has fewer and fewer citizens who are aware of their rights and duties and are willing to demonstrate this in a sustained and constructive manner in their everyday lives. This book is also premised on the imperative need in India to build a civil society, and a more *caring* and *humane* society, where the interests of the individual are harmonized with the concerns of the society.

Finally, this book has its inspiration in the overriding need for governance in India to improve, and it is our conviction that this can never happen unless citizens in their own self-interest are willing to *demand* better governance and know how to do so effectively.

This book is also in the nature of a beginning. It throws up ideas but does not claim to provide a comprehensive blueprint. We are aware that we may be accused of being idealistic and utopian. We are also aware that not all the ideas mentioned in this book will be able to cut through the pervasive haze of cynicism that has enshrouded much of the Indian middle class. And yet, we believe that the options before us are very limited. Either we pause and introspect and change *in our own long-term self-interest*, or we should be prepared to accept that such interests will never fructify as we have conceived them. We see this book, therefore, as a first step that could possibly initiate change in at least some people. For us this is enough.

I have greatly enjoyed co-authoring this book with Renuka Khandekar. I am grateful to her for her infectious optimism, in spite of personal odds which she always tried very hard to camouflage. I will always cherish this experience of working with her, even if she will never be able to forgive me for nagging her about not being able to reach her whenever she decided to suddenly leave for Uzbekistan (?!), or move bag and baggage to Bombay!

As always, my personal salutations to David Davidar and to Penguin. Both Renuka and I are also indebted to Ravi Singh who helped give form to this book.

PAVAN K. VARMA

*

It your throat constricts when the national anthem plays or your eyes overflow watching old patriotic film songs, you'll understand why we tried to cobble together a few ideas about Indian life in this book. It hurts so much to think how good it could have been.

We all mourn the passage to grief from those early nation-building years when our country began painfully to square her long-bowed shoulders. Why did we not stanch the blood sooner? How could we have let our lives go so completely off the rails? But we're not totally wrecked yet. Every week in our news magazines we read about people like us who make a difference, simply because their *manas* (mind-heart) wills them to positive action. Such people are living proof that India is at heart a loving, giving place, worth calling Home. But only if we work together can the difference that these remarkable people make show enough.

I have to concede (very reluctantly, but truth compels) that 'wording together' has been a fraught experience for my hapless, though gallant, co-author. *Mashallah*, his life flows majestically like the Ganga through the plains. Mine is like the Sutlej or Shatadru, rushing headlong in a hundred directions. Perhaps we are a metaphor for reconciling opposites, like so much else in India. My loving thanks to Pavan and Renu for the affection and concern heaped on me: I was actually tracked down to the heart of Asia, right to the middle of a fascinatmg pow-wow with the Imam Khatib of Tashkent, who was telling me Sufi stories. Thanks also to my

friend and former senior correspondent, Vandana
Malhotra, who got me just what I wanted in the
Zena article that sparked off this book. David,
thank you (though I know you'll make a face and
say, 'For what?!') and as for you, dear Ravi, your
patience deserves a *swarna kamal*.

Unabashedly,
Jai Hind

RENUKA KHANDEKAR

1

Why Bother?

If the times seem exceptionally difficult and the future exceptionally uncertain, dismiss the notion that the times and the future were ever anything else. There were always wars, there were always slumps, there were always crises . . . History, had it no other uses, would be valuable for this lesson alone—that man can cope with anything and that, from time to time, he will have to.

> —Parry's of Madras, A Story of British
> Enterprise in India, Hilton Brown

Why bother?

Why indeed must we, the educated middle class, bother with the socio-political mess that putrefies the outer edges of our hardworking lives?

Isn't urban India by itself said to constitute the third largest country in the world? Surely, then, we are entitled to form a separate republic by ourselves and reconstitute the clean, green, well-fed, well-maintained India we deserve for our ambitious personal efforts? If only . . .

If only those hateful others could be banished— ugly, dirty, poor and always defecating in public. How are *we* responsible for their stupidity, their unwillingness to study, to produce fewer children, to get vaccinated, to bathe, to comb their hair? Look how they spoil *our* lives!

After all, while we may all be equal in God's eyes, we are not so in each others'. Some of us are simply born more advantaged, even if our struggle thereafter to build our lives is no less arduous than anybody else's.

So what do people like us, who know of better ways to live, do with a country like ours? One, it is so overwhelmingly big. Two, it breeds one-seventh of all the people on the planet. Three, and most pernicious of all, it has so many of those unwashed others who refuse to go away.

Given these monstrous odds that we must overcome, where are the seven-league boots of the fairy tale, the fix-all yogi, the magic healer? Alas, nowhere except in our collective imagination.

It is wishful thinking of the most self-delusive (and therefore self-abusive) kind to hope for a *deus ex machina*, a 'god descending from a machine' to resolve a crisis, that the ancient Greeks had in their plays and that we ourselves are conditioned to expect by our folklore, myth and cinema. The truth is that our options are limited, and we had better grasp this truth very quickly:

- No messiah or leader with a magic wand will suddenly appear to change things overnight.

- No political revolution, like the one which caused an upheaval in China or, earlier, in the Soviet Union, is likely to occur now and unleash seismic changes in the structure of our society, making it unnecessary for *us* to do anything in the matter.

- The famous percolation theory of economics will not work. The system won't unclog itself enough for sufficient economic benefits to reach the huge numbers of the poor. However optimistic the economic model, the simple fact is that by the year 2025, the middle class—that is *us*—will alone have grown to around 500 million, and the poor and the absolutely deprived will still be swarming at a staggering 600 million.

■ There will be no sudden revolution in technology that will, like a fat-loss pill that promises results *without* dieting and exercise, activate productive solutions to India's problems without any effort on our part.

So what is going to happen? Is it the beginning of the end of civilization as we know it?

The symptoms of crisis will, of course, reveal themselves sooner than most of us expect. Don't believe it? Pay a short visit to Nairobi. It has oases of affluence just like us—hotels, casinos, restaurants, shopping malls, nice homes and gardens. But after 6.30 in the evening, you need an armed guard to go out.

That's because 47 per cent of the people in Kenya live below the poverty line. Thirty years ago the well-to-do citizens of Nairobi thought this wouldn't affect their lives. Now they lament that they have become prisoners of their own affluence, that they have, by turning their backs on their poor, created a society where the law of the jungle prevails.

It's happening in South Africa too, where 38 to 40 per cent of the people are unemployed. However prosperous some people in Johannesburg may be, the most pervasive sign in that city or anywhere else in the country is that of the security services.

So the first truth to understand is that we cannot insulate our lives from what is going on around us. And what might that be? Consider the facts:

- As many as 300 million people, more than the combined population of USA, Canada and bits of West Europe, go hungry to bed every night in our country. This is not fake scaremongering. It is a Planning Commission statistic, derived from that stark measurement known as the poverty line.

- Hovering on the brink of the poverty line are another 300 million people. One breadwinner's death, one accident or illness, and the entire family drops below the poverty line.

- Thus, in a nation of about one billion, we have 650 million people—more than the combined population of Europe and the Americas—who are trapped in sub-human conditions.

- The UNICEF report says that India will be the world's most illiterate country in the year 2000—that is 290 million illiterates, once again more than the combined population of USA and Canada.

- Seventy-five million Indian children below the age of five are malnourished. This means that more than half of all Indian children are malnourished—a rate worse than Ethiopia's (a country of 49 million people with a traumatic history of war and multi-colonial exploitation).

- Each year two million Indian babies—almost twice the population of Mauritius—die before their first birthday.

- Every *three minutes*, a child dies in India of something as easily curable as diarrhoea.

- Close to 60 per cent of all Indians do not have access to domestic lighting.

- Seventy-seven per cent have no access to tap water.

- About 60 per cent have no access to pucca houses.

- The rural female illiteracy rate is as high as 70 per cent. Only 15 per cent of Scheduled Caste women in Uttar Pradesh and Bihar can read or write their names.

- A staggering 98 per cent of rural India has no access to toilets.

If the facts are so overwhelming, why is it that we do not bother or notice?

Most middle-class people consider themselves to be educated, articulate, sophisticated, suave—the end products of a 5,000-year-old civilizational continuity. Why is it then that we do not notice? Why is it that we have convinced ourselves that these statistics are too spectacular to be true, that they belong to some other place, some other country, some other planet, anywhere else but India? In fact, statistics have stopped meaning anything to us. To people like us, the truth about India is only that it is the world's largest democracy (which it is), that it has one of the world's largest reservoirs of skilled manpower (which in absolute numbers it does), that it has notched up achievements in the frontier areas of technology (also true), and that it is a nation that rejoices in the world's largest middle class.

Armed with such image-restoring placards, the educated Indian middle class has just stopped noticing. The amazing fact is that the truth stares us in the face at our very doorstep:

- Roughly 40 per cent of Delhi is a slum according to the government statistics.

- Fifty per cent of Mumbai, a city that dares to call itself *Urbs Prima in Indis*, or India's First City, is *visibly* a slum. It has to be middle-class India's weirdest joke that Mumbai professionals (notably in media, advertising and commerce—the Articulate Empowered?) delude themselves, as they totter out of wannabe-West pubs, that 'Mumbai is like New York'. Another oft-heard Mumbai mantra is: 'We have *systems* for everything—from lunchboxes to the retrieval of impounded cars.' The truth is

Mumbaikars live in one of the ugliest and most polluted cities on the planet, and because they cannot afford a flat in the crowded metropolis, they spend more than half their lives commuting to town from the suburbs and back.

- As many as 35 per cent of the people in Delhi, the capital of India, defecate in the open.

- A staggering 40 per cent of the capital of India is illiterate.

- Fifteen hundred tonnes of garbage remains unlifted every day from Delhi. The same degree of filth can be seen in any other big city in India.

But middle-class India does not register what any foreigner does not stop noticing, that there is something very wrong around us which needs some very urgent solutions.

One of our favourite beliefs is that over population is the only culprit. Reduce the number of the unwashed masses and all will be well. True. But how do we go about doing this? If it was

possible in a functioning democracy to forcibly
sterilize the vast millions of the poor—'those' people
who are dragging us down with their mindless
poverty and slums and squalor—then many of us
would agree that this is the best policy. But the
problem is that it is not possible to pursue such a
policy. It was tried once in the past and it failed.

Nor is it the best policy. Human beings cannot
be treated as commodities, to be trimmed and
pruned as *we* would like to see them. The real
answer to India's over population lies in increasing
the spread of primary education, health care and,
above all, and *dramatically*, female literacy. In the
absence of basic education, not only are the majority
of Indians unable to take decisions for their own
long term good, they also do not even understand
the government's propaganda on the need for family
planning.

But mass education will not bring us immediate
results, nor do people like us believe that it is even
a foolproof method. We want everything in a hurry,
and we want it only for ourselves.

Most of us believe that the ideal solution to
everything is to build a fortress around our little
worlds. Many of us valiantly make the attempt. We
are willing to bribe the linesman so long as *we* get

electricity. We are willing to put a booster on the main water line in order to fill our *own* water tank. We are willing to ignore garbage just outside our gate so long as our *own* premises are clean.

But the truth is that such private fortresses are no longer sustainable. Islands unto themselves are sinking with an entire system going under. The number of such fortresses may increase but the ground beneath their ramparts is being cut away by the sheer ineffectiveness of the system as a whole.

There is, therefore, no solution but to bother and to be concerned about what is happening around us. The imperative need is to be committed. To begin the transition from being merely *residents* to being *citizens*. This engagement does not require a dramatic sacrifice. There is no need for any one to become a full-time social worker, renouncing family and comforts. There is no need for any one of us to be a Mahatma.

What is required is a pragmatic revolution where ordinary people—people like us—begin to get concerned. For this, we don't need role models so exalted and self-sacrificing that they actually put us off by being too unreal for us. We don't need people whom we cannot even *hope* to emulate. We need to check out or connect with ordinary people who resemble us, who have dreams, faults and ambitions like we have, but *in addition*, they possess that profound quality of *involvement* that we ourselves could not or did not allow to develop into social concern and sensitivity.

In any case, continuing to lead our lives as if nothing is wrong is to be worse than an ostrich with its head firmly under layers of sand. But even if we agree to pull our heads out of the sand and begin to notice what is wrong and what needs to be done, can our involvement ever make a difference when the problems are so vast and the remedies so inadequate? The answer to this is an emphatic yes. There are no other options, as we have discussed before. The important thing is to understand that an individual matters and that his or her contribution, however small, *can* make a difference.

Later, in the chapter titled 'Squirrels at Setu', we will give examples to show that individual stories of care and concern have made a visible difference to the lives of people. These are true stories. But they are too few in number. If such stories of individual care and concern can multiply a hundred or a thousand times, gradually the face of India will begin to change.

Most important, it is only when individuals begin to be concerned that *governance* can begin to improve. The country is crying out for a revolution in governance. The policies are in place, we have some of the best laws in the world, but their implementation is one of the poorest on the planet. And if we are honest, we have been partners in this entire exercise of subversion. One example will suffice to prove this point. Less than 5 per cent of urban India pays taxes, and 70 per cent of the top 1,500 Indian companies pay zero tax. The 1998 Global Competitiveness Report ranks India as among the top five countries noted for tax evasion. Some estimates put the quantum of tax evasion to be as high as almost 20 per cent of our Gross Domestic Product. If we do not pay our taxes, how can we expect the government to implement its laws?

We can continue to apportion blame: it is not us, we maintain, but the politicians; not us, insist the politicians, but the bureaucrats; not us, the bureaucrats can say, but the businessmen. But this is an endless, sterile argument. And we do not have the indulgence of time anymore.

The truth is that when citizens want, a system can be made to work. And when a system works, it

brings about improvements in the quality of the
lives of all concerned, including our own. Good
governance, indeed, is the key. But good governance
requires good citizens who bother. The time has
come, therefore, for the middle and elite classes to
pause, to introspect, and to think. Not on the
grounds of idealism, not because this is what they
are supposed to do, not because somebody has
asked them to do so, but because this is in their
own long-term self-interest.

This book's proposed agenda is for national
redressal as a practical, corporate act by us, the
shareholders of Bharat Inc. At the basic level, it is
about a private-public interaction between a people
and their state, a willingness to pay for our lives as
grown-ups.

We may be the world's largest democracy, but
we have very few citizens. The stark truth is that
unless we drag, push, pull that 'horrible' other
India with us, unless we, the educated minority,
make our country work—for us *and* them—we might
as well book seats on those new passenger
spaceships that the Americans are working on.
Because we must remember that societies which
have a great degree of economic inequality are also
highly unstable politically. And political instability

can very seriously jeopardize that very security and economic prosperity that we seek.

The bottom line is that there really is nowhere to go. This is the only country we have and all those others are here to stay with us. They have nowhere else to go either. It is like being born into an enormous joint family. Either we all swim, or we sink. We need a new agenda for action because the way we are going we are half into the water with no lifeboats around. Not believing the truth will not help anymore.

Most people sense this. They are fed up with living solely at the level of wants irrespective of the means, of accepting the immoral, of living with compromise, of adjusting to the betrayal of faith. There is a future there for all of us, but only if we see our own roles beyond our own little horizons. People want change, and they want to change. In small and big ways this book is a beginning towards that all important—and unavoidable—endeavour that has to be pursued in our own interest by *all* of us.

2

Sarkari Vows

Freedom and progress can be experienced only by the individual; not by any collectivity such as a nation or class.

Man is therefore the measure of things—freedom and progress in society can be assessed only as the freedom and progress of individuals.

No democratic order is possible which does not place the individual at the centre of things.

—M.N. Roy

Did you know that there's a 234-page-fat publication printed by the Government of India Press, Minto Road, New Delhi-110 002, that proclaims itself to be the Annual Report,

Government of India, Ministry of Social Justice & Empowerment?

Written in dry, *sarkari* language, the promise it holds within its pages is nevertheless exciting stuff, because it contains the good intentions of the Republic of India towards its citizens, including the more disadvantaged. Obtaining a glimpse of these intentions and decoding them, however, are sterner tasks than a citizen might imagine.

The latest such document (1997-98) describes the mandate of the ministry, its policy and approach:

The Ministry of Social Justice & Empowerment is entrusted with the welfare, social justice and empowerment of disadvantaged and marginalized sections of the society, viz. Scheduled Castes, Scheduled Tribes, Minorities, Backward Classes, Disabled, Aged Persons, Street Children, Victims of Drug Abuse etc. During the IVth Plan period a beginning was made to extend economic development parallel to social empowerment. This was resolved through viable institutions for extending credit at low interest to families under double the Poverty Line.

The basic objective of the policies, programmes, laws and institutions of the Indian Welfare System

is to bring the target groups into the mainstream
of development *by making them self-reliant*.
(Emphasis ours).

Two paragraphs down, the document says, with
disarming honesty,

The programmes and schemes of the Ministry
address about 85 per cent of the total population
of the country. However, there remains an
unbridgeable gap between the resources at the
disposal of the Ministry and the magnitude of
the tasks envisaged.

Like our venerable Constitution, this document
too is a testament to the state's faith in and
commitment to the people. It's all there in the
blueprint. What, then, creates an 'unbridgeable
gap' between the word and the deed? Corrupt,
unhelpful officials? But the worst of them, like the
best of us, are merely people. The law, which was
there before them and, hopefully, will be there long
after they vacate their official chairs, is
unequivocally on our side.

It comes down then to the basic truth that
Information is Power. The obstructive creature on

the other side of that municipal desk knows things
we don't. He blocks our information and therefore
our access to action. It's the oldest trick in the
book, in the history of any civilization, regime or
mindset.

To beat this poisonous system of 'non-
cooperation' and take what is legally and morally
ours, we have to A) know our rights and B) demand
them, quoting chapter and verse from the relevant
book of rules.

The overriding need to do this is naturally
linked to our self-interest. But it is also related to
a larger issue: the need, across the board, to improve
governance, and revitalize existing *sarkari*
institutions which have absorbed a great deal of
the resources of the national exchequer but rarely
deliver well on their mandated tasks.

A few random facts will establish how wrong
things really are:

- In India, out of every rupee of revenue that
  the state governments receive, almost 60
  paise are taken up by wages and salaries of
  state employees.

- A study has established that while

government expenditure in South Asia has more than doubled from $1.25 in 1975 to $1.56 in 1995, the number of people in poverty has increased from 270 million in the 1960s to over 515 million in 1995.

■ Similarly, while the central governments' expenditure in South Asia as a part of the total budget has increased from 14 per cent to more than 17 per cent in the last 25 years, amazingly, the number of illiterate adults has grown from 280 million to 395 million during the same period.

■ In India, not only has the government apparatus grown inefficiently, it continues to remain bewilderingly complex. For instance, it requires 47 different approvals to construct a building in Mumbai, and a small-scale entrepreneur has to deal with as many as 36 inspectors each month and fill up 46 different documents!

The losses incurred by such an inefficient *sarkari* establishment are huge. They affect us and our lives. Consider these facts:

■ As per 1998 statistics, non-performing loans made by public banks amounted to as much as 18 per cent of their total advances.

■ The losses of state electricity boards in India are equivalent to a staggering 24 per cent of the country's GDP as per statistics available for 1998. (In fact, systems losses in South Asia power utilities are set twice as high as those anywhere else in the world.)

■ The Integrated Rural Development Programme has leakages which range from 20 per cent to 50 per cent.

■ More than half of the beneficiaries of the public distribution system are estimated to be not the intended beneficiaries, but the non-poor.

■ Only about 40 per cent of the total wheat supply reaches the poorest 40 per cent of the Indian people in spite of a wide governmental infrastructure to ensure fair distribution.

Much of this dismal state of affairs will, as certainly as the sun rising from the east, affect our long-term good. A recent World Bank study has shown that a country with an inefficient bureaucracy and the consequent inevitable policy distortions will have an annual growth rate that is seven times lower than that of relatively well governed countries.

It is clear that such a state of affairs continues because of our inability to hold the system accountable through the informed assertion of our rights as tax payers (alas, that there were more!), and a systemic and sustained projection of outrage and indignation as citizens.

Given the extent of the official machinery, and the number and complexity (often deliberate) of government departments, as also the loopholes which allow them to flourish in inefficiency, making government institutions accountable is not an easy task. However, a beginning must be made, and it is best made in ensuring better services in those government departments that function in areas which concern our everyday lives.

The point of this chapter is to persuade you of the absolute need to assert your rights as a consumer, be it of public or private services (and goods). The hope is that coming generations will acquire this important confidence. We have to learn to demand that institutions perform in our interests.

And information about their duties (which are our rights) is the first step.

To begin with, every city corporation has to live by its charter, which includes a list of its officials at various levels of seniority who can be contacted for the redress of complaints. Their names and phone numbers are meant to be listed and the list must be made available to the public. While this is an interesting fact, our readers may think, of what real use is it? How will a citizen ever access such a list, presuming, of course, that it has been compiled at all? While the scope of this book is indicative and cannot be exhaustive at an all-India level, we are proud and happy to bring to your attention a pioneering initiative in this direction. In concert with the *Indian Express*, Praja, an NGO in Mumbai, brought out the Citizen's Charter of The Municipal Corporation of Greater Mumbai in June 1999.

The Praja team consists of Nitai Mehta, Ashok Jogani, Sumangali Gada, Ajay Hattangadi, Sunil Alva, Ashish Wanjira, Smita Kothari, Gavin De Sa, Anuj Bhojwani, Samantha Saldanha and Apurv Muthalia. You can visit them at HYPERLINK 'http:/ /www.praja.org/' www.praja.org or email them at HYPERLINK 'mailto:praja-foundation@hotmail' praja-foundation@hotmai.com. Their postal address is PRAJA, PO Box 16079, Colaba Post Office, Wodehouse Road, Mumbai 400 005.

So what have these concerned citizens done with the help of a socially committed national daily?

What these people have done is exemplary. They are all busy professionals in an indubitably stressful city like Mumbai. But by each lending his or her shoulder to the wheel, they have, hopefully, set in motion a Chetna Jagran, or awakening of awareness, that must and shall empower those who now know not only their rights as citizens, but also how to assert them.

We use the analogy of the wheel instinctively, for does it not turn deep in our national psyche as the embodiment of progress and movement? Think of our tricolour and the Ashoka Chakra it proudly bears. This important national emblem derives from the Buddha's first ever sermon. It was called thereafter the Dharma Chakra Parivartana—that which set in motion the Wheel of Law.

And so this deed, of compiling a citizen's charter centuries later, resonates in our minds with the spirit of empowerment that once lit this very land—curiously enough, when there were republican systems of government around, like in ancient Vaishali.

The Law that argued passionately then for Right Action was not mere soul talk. It was and is a clarion call to Do The Right Thing, even—especially!—in the mundane workings of daily life. It translates into unlovely but essential concerns like water, electricity, waste disposal.

Take a look at the departments listed on the contents page of the Praja-Express Citizen's Charter (Did you even know there were such bodies? We didn't, till we began this book!):

- Solid Waste Management

- Waterworks

- Storm Water Drains

- Road Maintenance

- Public Health

- BEST/Traffic

- Licences

- Environment

- Education

- Sewerage Operations

- Complaint Procedure: simple, step-by-step directions

- Appendices (names and telephone numbers of relevant officials)

Finally, there is an invitation to link up with the Praja-Express initiative (refer addresses above).

Once Praja was established, with the clearly expressed mandate of enabling citizens to know their rights in order to ensure better governance, local officialdom responded positively. For instance, Hareshwar Patil, the Mayor of Mumbai, stated quite clearly the reason for Town Hall's support: 'We are very interested in maintaining a higher standard of public services.'

K. Nalinakshan, the Municipal Commissioner, Municipal Corporation of Greater Mumbai (MCGM) spells out the principles on which a Citizen's Charter is based:

1. Standards: The citizens are aware of the quality of services that can be expected of the MCGM and take prescribed action if the services do not conform to these standards.

2. Accountability: Through the Citizen's Charter,

a clear line of responsibility for the various services (is) established.

3. Transparency: Information that is relevant to the people's needs is offered so as to ensure their participation in civic life.

4. Feedback: The MCGM looks forward to the citizens using this document as we will then get an accurate response as to how effectively the public services met their needs.

And B.G. Deshmukh, former Home Secretrary to the Union Government, presently Chairman of the Tata Council for Community Initiatives, is worth quoting for the direct hits aimed at all of us:

Efficient city administration is a function of several inter-linked factors, one of the most important being the quality of intelligent citizenship. A good local self-government cannot function with just a highly motivated beaureaucracy and elected representatives alone. The other side of the coin is the concern, awareness and interest manifested by the city's inhabitants. An enlightened and well-informed citizen body can pressure the local government body into action and compel it to respond to the needs of the people.

Democracy is the only form of government that allows citizens full and free expression. It bestows a power which is really quite impotent unless it is used. Of course, the exercise of this power needs enlightened citizens who are driven by a sense of social responsibility.

Lethargy and indifference are the food on which misgovernment and corruption thrive. The essence of an efficient civic administration is, therefore, an enlightened, active community.

What makes us sit up and take notice is the repeated use of the word 'enlightened'. For the burden of our song, in this book and in every private and public forum, is 'elightened self-interest'. Do it because it's good for you.

Since India is too vast and varied to yet standardize a National Manual (though we should one day!), we stress again that the scope of this chapter can at best be indicative of how a big Indian city organizes its services. In detailing the information below, it is our purpose to acquaint you with the theoretical workings of the blueprint. It is a glimpse into the internal municipal machinery of Mumbai city, which is not just our commercial hub but a true cosmopolis, where almost every

region and community of India is represented like
nowhere else, except of course the capital.

So just by way of example, here's what you
need to know in the small but smelly matter of
Mumbai's garbage disposal (officially known as Solid
Waste Management):

Pecking Order:

- Chief Engineer

- Deputy Engineers

- Head Supervisors of city zones (report to
  Chief Engineer)

- Assistant Head Supervisor responsible at
  ward level (in Mumbai) for garbage disposal.

Functions:

- Sweeping of public roads

- Maintenance of public toilets

- Disposal of solid waste and animal carcasses

- Sanitary measures to keep the city clean

How Soon Should The Solid Waste Management Ward Office Respond To Your Complaint? Depending on the nature of the complaint, the ward office promises appropriate action within a period ranging from 24 hours to eight days.

Within 24 hours for:

- Garbage not lifted from authorized collection spot

- Collection points not attended properly

- Garbage lorry not covered

- Sweeping of roads

- Removal of dead animals

Within 48 hours for:

- No attendants at public toilets

Within 8 days for:

- Providing/replacing garbage bins

(*Note:* Though it's not this department's

responsibility to clean the gullies between or behind houses, it does in fact perform this task. It is, thus, our responsibility as residents to ensure that we don't dump rubbish in our back lanes.)

Turning now to the Mumbai Waterworks Department, you can demand action within

Two to seven days (allowance for digging permission delay) for:

■ Leaks in water line

24 hours for:

■ Burst water lines
■ Contaminated water supply

48 hours for:

■ Water shortage
■ Tanker permission (apply to the Deputy Hydraulics Engineer)

Seven days for:

■   Test results of defective meters

And here's how you apply for a permanent water connection:

1. Get application form from the ward office between 1030 and 1500 hrs

2. The ward office acknowledges your submitted form between 1030 and 1500 hrs.

3. They tell you if there's some error in your form within seven days.

4. A month later they inspect your 'site', get the official sanction and issue permission.

5. Other departments give you clearance certificates, the work is certified and you're asked to pay four days later

6. The Assistant Engineer permits you to dig the road four days after you apply to him with your other documents.

The Waterworks Department gets to fine you if you:

- Misuse fire hydrants

- Take an unauthorized water connection

- Install an unauthorized loft tank

- Use a booster pump

- Don't keep your overhead tank clean

- Pretend to be someone else and use their connection

To get an Electricity Connection in Mumbai and most other Indian cities, follow these steps:

1. Get an application form at the local Electric Supply Undertaking office.

2. Fill and submit, with required documents.

3. Get the application receipt when you submit it.

4. They tell you the same day if you've made a mistake or your application is incomplete.

5. Get the Test Report of the licensed electrical contractor done.

6. They give you your NOC (No Objection

Certificate) in a month if a sub-station isn't required and the estimate for a service cable, meter board and sanctions for these.

7. You pay a deposit of Rs 50 pkw (per kilowatt) for homes, colleges and hospitals, non-profit trusts, religious institutions and homes rented as offices/shops. All other tariffs are Rs 150 pkw.

8. Getting the cable to your home happens in a month, except in the rains.

9. You pay a Connection Fee of Rs 150 pkw for residences and Rs 300 pkw for other purposes. In Mumbai, charitable, religious and medical institutions are not exempted from tax under the BMC act.

If you have billing complaints, go with a hard copy of the bill to the superintendent of your zonal Consumers' Department. They have to set it right in seven days!

For other hassles, go to the supervisor, wards.

Each city corporation/ public service department has its own indulgences and facilities for citizens.

It is truly worth your while to march in and ask for
a copy of the charter of each department—just look
up your local water or electricity board office in the
directory, and likewise for other departments,
including those two important ones: telephones and
insurance!

Here's a typical list of important public service
departments for New Delhi:

- New Delhi Municipal Corporation

- Municipal Corporation of Delhi

- Delhi Development Authority

- Central Public Works Department

- Delhi Vidyut Board

- Delhi Jal Board

- Mahanagar Telephone Nigam Ltd

- Ministry of Urban Affairs & Employment

- Ministry of Petroleum & Natural Gas Oil
  Coordination Committee

- Central Board of Excise & Customs

- Ministry of Railways

■   Public Distribution System, Ministry of Civil
    Supplies

Do make it your business to collect such
charters, read, analyse and understand their import
and *share* the information as well as devise
strategies for action. To start you off, we give below
a sequence of steps for action. They differ from the
civic responses detailed in the chapter that follows—
'Fighting Injustice'. The points below are civic
initiatives, for us to get started on the business of
making our lives work. God and Government have
both empowered us with the absolute luck of a
democratic state.

The only thing that can restore our energy
before we lose our wits completely, is perspective:
we have chosen the long, slow democratic path,
because it is humane and inclusive. It is our core
value, as we all know deep in our hearts. It is the
value sung by our saints, poets and reformers, it is
the value embodied in the shining person we call
the Mahatma, the Father of our nation, whom we
just overwhelmingly voted as our Man of the
Millennium.

It is fashionable these days to laugh at Gandhi,
at his experiments with sexual abstinence, his

human failings. But have you visited Westminster in London? Those still-awesome buildings must have seemed truly terrifying when they were the centre of the world's largest Empire. Yet this frail old man, this 'naked fakir', brought it all tumbling down. How did he begin? By picking up a broom and cleaning a toilet! Armed with nothing but a sense of right. That's why our grandfathers flocked to adore him. That's why our protected grandmothers came out on the streets and let themselves be beaten up by lathis. We don't have to do such drastic things. But we can at least produce enough energy to manage our own lives better. Hence this practical action plan:

1. Make a master list of important services. The daily newspapers print some of these in any case: police, fire, ambulance, airports, railways and so on.

2. Add to that list, with some help from your local Yellow Pages, the names, addresses and phone numbers—and the names of personal assistants!—of:

   ■ municipal corporators

- municipal departments

- the chief reporter/city editor and chief photographer of local and national newspapers, so you can inform the city desk of longstanding neighbourhood civic sorrows.

3. Collect the charters of the Jal Board, the Vidyut Board, the Municipal Corporation, the Department of Horticulture, Ministry of Posts and Telegraphs, the telephone authorities and other such relevant bodies.

4. Make copies of these documents and distribute to each office bearer of your residents' association.

5. Ask the association to undertake the expense of making copies for each home in the colony, with key sections highlighted.

6. Once this is done, devise a schedule for discussion of each charter amongst the residents. Let the meetings not degenerate into occasions for oratory, but set a proper agenda with a time-frame.

7. Through these meetings, arrive at a

consensus on a task list of priorities for your neighbourhood.

8. Divide the task list among volunteer task forces. One group can tackle the water seepage problem. Another can take up the planting of trees. A third group can address garbage clearance. A fourth can set up security systems. A fifth can organize a pressure group to get the colony roads re-tarred. And so on.

9. Set up regular meetings to report on progress to each other. Have a general discussion period wherein ideas and strategies can be pooled, to enable each other's work. It is important to encourage each other, especially if it turns out that one such group accomplishes its goal faster than the rest. Otherwise, initiative will die. Remember, it is a common battle being fought on several fronts and there is no shame in sharing genuine difficulties and asking for tips from each other.

10. When your association achieves something, disseminate this information to other

groups: your kitty/hobby group or professional association. Share the entire process, from how your colony identified a task to the steps taken to achieve it, the pitfalls and perils en route and the response to each problem. Write this down: you are compiling a historic social document, an *astra* of change, no less. Others can study your methods and activate them too.

11. Take help from those who have struggled before you: invite a lawyer or activist who has engaged in such work to talk to your association on ways and means. Ask them to put your association in touch with other associations.

When these steps have been accomplished, aim at organizing a ward association meet: the individual residents' associations in a neighbourhood can convene to formulate a ward action plan for civic redressal. This can be the foundation of a priceless citizen's network that can spread from area to area of your city.

In particular, it is important to co-opt the residents of poorer colonies, treat their representatives with honour and respect and make them equal partners in our initiative. This means doing several things that matter very much in Indian society and culture. Like offering them a seat and refreshment without patronizing them, talking matter-of-factly and sensibly about the benefits of concerted action and *most importantly*, not sounding accusatory with hurtful words like 'Your colony is the dirtiest', 'You people don't know how to live', and so on. Always use words like 'Our city', 'Our problems', 'Our children', 'Our future'. We can't endure it when affluent foreigners speak patronizingly to us. How can we then disdain our own people, just because we earn more or know more?

If after doing all this you get no response within the period stipulated in the charter, or if someone there wants a bribe or is rude, don't lose your cool straight away. Persevere.

As far as using the media to achieve your rightful ends goes, here are a few tips: Without saying why, find out the name and designation of the offending clerk or official, make a note of the time, date, place, your request and his response. Write/type it out without exaggeration and then call the newspaper. You have a better chance of being heard if you organize your facts beforehand. News desks are besieged night and day by all kinds of nut cases or just vicious troublemakers trying to frame others. So, a rational approach that meets them halfway with properly laid-out facts, and contacting the right person (see point 2 above), gets a better response than if you call in the white heat of rage. And don't imagine the papers are not interested, they are!

The press, despite everything you hear maligning the scribe tribe, is a pillar of our democratic identity. What we, as alert citizens, must keep in mind, however, is that everyone succumbs to certain mindsets. In our collective case, it is to unilaterally blame the government for all our woes. Let's not forget that the government is staffed by middle-class Indians, by people drawn from our ranks, people like you and me. The point we'd like to emphasize is that we do have these structures and systems already, so let's make them work for us by first finding out *how* they're supposed to function. And let us not take away credit from the many sincere and upright bureaucrats struggling amongst those corrupt others to improve the state of the nation with the power accorded to them.

If we don't take the initiative to make our

sarkar deliver, we will stay stuck forever as whingers and whiners. As journalist Manini Chatterjee wrote in a January book review in *India Today*, '. . . attacking statism has become the new orthodoxy. From the World Bank to Booker Prize winners to chirpy young Star News reporters, everyone's favourite target is the state and politicians. But a caring civil society cannot be built on the ruins of a democratic state. Nor can the government be made more accountable by decrying its very existence.'

To put it very simply indeed, warts and all, it is *our* government, the one *we* elected. The reasons for its arrogance and autocracy are many: suffice to say, the colonial legacy and our own long history of servitude are the chief villains of this tragedy. *Training* our *sarkar* to deliver, alas, then devolves on us as enlightened citizens, until the government fulfils its appointed role as our servant. There's no escape from this particular karmic duty!

3

How to Fight Injustice

Fear in citizens is the enemy of freedom from domestic misrule. Dear reader, whatever your age and profession may be, do not murder the truth that rises from time to time in your heart.

—Rajaji,
Swarajya, 14 May 1966

If a citizen were to be defined by his or her ability to stand up against injustice and illegality, a very large segment of the Indian middle class would not qualify. Though we have matured as participants in a democracy, and are aware of our rights in deciding the fate of governments and political parties, we seem to have shrunk as citizens in our abilities to confront wrong.

This has happened over the years. We have come to see the public-spirited citizen who is willing to stick his neck out when he sees wrong, as a long-suffering idealist, embittered and harassed, a lone voice in the wilderness, destined to be ultimately pulverized into conformity.

We are convinced that there is little purpose served in taking a stand. The system overwhelms us. Its corruption staggers us. The might of the establishment frightens us. We are reconciled to being mute witnesses to the sway of misrule. We accept and therefore are compromised.

The result is that we have become silent accessories to our own daily abuse and debasement. We do nothing, though we see it all: the high-handedness, the criminal negligence, the abuse of authority, the callous lack of rightful response from authority, the flaunting of power, the blatant breaking of rules and, finally, shatteringly, our own humiliation as the end-users of the system.

If we pause to look, this death dance enacts itself in our everyday lives. If we need an electricity connection, we are willing to compromise with the system rather than assert our rights as the end-users. If we are aware of somebody putting a water pump directly on the main line supplying water, we are reluctant to fight as long as our own tank is somehow filled. When we see those with influence using their clout to admit their children in schools while those with merit are refused admission, we rarely give vent to our indignation in the shape of an effective protest. If the garbage piles up where it should not, we rarely confront the authorities through collective action. When we see illegal constructions coming up with the visible collusion of the authorities, we do not think it *our* business to voice a protest.

We are equally mute when we see the vandalization of public parks, the encroachments on footpaths and the misuse of public land in market places. When we see a policeman taking a bribe, we rarely stop to censure him. We accept VIP quotas, the inefficiency of public bodies, the inexcusable delays in flights, the arrogance of VIP motorcades, the affront of absent *babus*, and the unacceptable arbitrariness of those whose job it is to provide us municipal services or collect our taxes.

The tragedy is that the more we remain silent, the more this becomes a way of life. We become not only victims but colluders. We are then not mere witnesses to wrongdoing, we become its facilitators. When we see wrong, we shut our eyes by reflex. We pay agencies that are in the wrong so that we may fulfil our own short-term needs, thus loosening one more brick from the crumbling edifice that is our system. Indeed, we almost look forward to the *corruptibility* of the system as a means to better avail of what it can offer *us*. The irony is that ultimately we are compelled to grease palms in order to obtain what is legitimately ours. And, of course, we are quite willing to grease them when we are seeking to acquire what is *not* legitimately ours.

The truth is that the citizen who is willing to take a stand to preserve the rectitude of the system has died. The whole system has begun to stink. Accountability has come to a near nought. The ideal citizen—which each one of us believes he or she is—has long ceased to exist, buried under the sands of inertia, guilt, collusion and cowardice.

What, therefore, can be done? How can each of us help salvage the situation? How can we draw from ourselves the resolve to take a stand, the courage that is required to begin the process of change? The task is not easy. In taking on the system, there is the flawed legacy of the last five

decades; there is the obvious strength of the
establishment or the wrongdoer; there is the
consciousness of individual fragility. There is no
alternative today but to begin tackling it. Here are
some thoughts on how we might do that:

The shaping of resolve: The first step is to make the
resolve to say *no* to wrongdoing when one sees it.

Recognizing the long-term damage: A simple
message must sink in—it is better to face the
consequences of sticking our neck out today than to
condemn ourselves, our children and family to face
worse consequences tomorrow.

The maturing of resolve: The answer lies not in
sporadic or dramatic tantrums. Hysteria is a sign
of weakness. The resolve must be calm, but edged
with steel. It must be an inflexible statement of
disapproval. It must be an unambiguous but
enduring assertion that what is unjust or wrong is
unacceptable. The maturing of such a resolve must
lead to the ability to protest, but with dignity and
quiet determination. It means hanging in there to
have our say.

Full knowledge of one's rights and duties: Each one

of us, as a citizen, has certain rights against authority. We must be aware of these. You'll find an indication of these rights in regard to government agencies in the chapter 'Sarkari Vows'. But we also have *duties* and these are important because none of us can protest against wrongdoing if we are not sensitive to the duties that devolve upon us as citizens.

Knowledge of remedies: All of us are aware that agencies with which we interface, mostly within the purview of the government, but also in the private realm, are required to keep complaint books. These are rarely used. Few people ask for them, and, as a result, even when asked for, they are not available. A complaint book is the first step to legitimately voicing your protest or grievance. It is a public document. It is useful to keep a copy of what you have noted in the complaint book. If you can't make a photocopy, retain the text or the broad gist of what you've written, and remember the date on which you lodged the complaint. If there is no action on a complaint, incorporate this text in a letter addressed to the chief of that organization. The important point is that we should convey to a wrongdoer that his or her misdemeanour will be challenged and pursued to its rightful conclusion.

Use of the media: Newspapers are often willing to make public instances of wrongdoing by officialdom or private agencies which have ridden roughshod over a consumer. Most papers now have city supplements. There is, in most papers, a grievance column. Contrary to what a lot of us may think, these do make an impact. There is nothing which irks an erring official more than to have his wrongdoing made public. He or she is then required to provide an explanation. Repeated protests in the media against such an official are a direct challenge to his misdemeanour. Often papers are willing to go beyond the space allocated for complaints and do a larger story. These have a definitive impact. A recent case was that of Dr Shreenath Gupta, a Reader in the Delhi School of Economics, who was unfairly harassed by the Delhi Police when he did not, for reasons quite beyond his control, move off the road immediately to accommodate a VIP motorcade. Gupta was issued a challan and his car was impounded. He then contacted a correspondent in the *Times of India*. The newspaper carried his story on its front page. There was quite an uproar at the manner in which he was dealt with. People came forward to fight his cause. A public interest litigation (PIL) was admitted in the Delhi High

Court. Other newspapers carried his story. He was interviewed on several television channels. The net result was that an individual was able to take on the system which he felt had wronged him.

The strength of residents' associations: Delhi is dotted with residents' associations, be they for apartment blocks or entire colonies. The strength of such associations is often underestimated. They represent a collective body of people whose representation cannot be ignored if effectively presented. Any one who is witness to injustice should seek to reinforce his or her own efforts to fight it by seeking the support of the association to which he or she belongs. These associations should also consider setting up a Special Cell to respond quickly to such appeals for help.

Other fora: You could also tap the support of bodies like the Rotary Club and the Lions Club, or NGOs who deal with specific cases of injustice. For instance, there are several NGOs dealing with the empowerment of women. There are organizations which seek to protect women from harassment. It is not difficult to identify such bodies and to enlist their support for a public cause.

Elected representatives: Parliament House in Delhi

may be the somewhat inaccessible apex forum overseeing our democracy, but elected representatives at different levels of the democratic structure are not difficult to reach. Right up there in the Lok Sabha is your local Member of Parliament. Under him, and nearer to you, there are elected MLAs. There are elected representatives of local bodies whose job it is to represent and protect your interests. These elected representatives have to win elections. They cannot ignore an effective, and better still, *collective* representation made to them against wrongdoing or injustice. Where their vested interests are involved, they may seek to scuttle a request for action, or bury a protest, or ignore a representation. But the pressure of the democratic process is such that if the protest refuses to die down, and is given even greater prominence by the media, it is likely that your local elected representative will intervene to rectify the wrong.

This is not a matter of giving credit where it is not due. We are aware of the pervasive perception that elected representatives do not care for their constituents once they are elected. However, the emphasis here is not on the idealism of the elected representative. The emphasis here is that he or she

will take cognizance of the need to intervene in
support of a cause against injustice in his or her
own self-interest, because the next election is never
too far away. The truth is that we have never ever
subjected our elected representatives to the
organized pressure of those they are supposed to
serve. If we do, it is more than likely that they will
be persuaded to deliver better to us, for now it is
their self-interest at stake!

Legal remedies: This, again, is a very neglected
area in terms of a citizen's usage. We have,
fortunately, an elaborate judicial system in place.
For a variety of reasons, it is often not the most
expedient or even the most effective. But apparently,
this is also because those who can benefit from it
do not resort to it for relief. Resorting to a legal
process is both a threat and a challenge to the
wrongdoer. It brings the act of wrongdoing and
injustice outside the private realm of the perpetrator
and the victim, to a public forum, to the wider
interests of all citizens. It is a good augury that the
judicial system is itself today more responsive to
complainants who seek legal relief against the high-
handedness or ineffectiveness of authorities. Several
new instruments have come into place such as the
Public Interest Litigation (PIL).

It is also necessary that lawyers provide free service to larger causes which affect their own well-being as citizens. Legal aid does exist in this country, but there is a need to go beyond that. Every bar association should have a core cell of lawyers who are willing to interface with a wronged citizen in order to be able to provide judicial relief to him or her. Even outside the bar association, individual lawyers who are at the top of their profession should set aside some time from their practice to take up such cases. Indeed, this should be one of the criteria to judge how successful a lawyer has become.

Organized monitoring: There is no substitute for the *vigilance* of citizens. If an official agency is aware that its work is being monitored and that alert citizens are keeping a report card on its performance, which they are willing to make public, the chances are that their misdemeanours will lessen. Residents' associations can easily set up a core group whose job is to monitor agencies such as the local branch of the municipal department, sanitary and sewage disposal authorities, the local electricity supply units, the police station and the local environment body.

The yardstick for such monitoring should be carefully devised, and then made public. The criteria could include politeness, responsiveness, efficiency, honesty, accessibility and so on. Such technical performance report cards by residents' associations could be made public every month, or on a regular basis.

Indeed, the need of the hour is for citizens to create and multiply anti-corruption watchdog bodies. The Independent Commission Against Corruption in Hong Kong is a good example of such a body. The Public Affairs Centre in Bangalore is another good role model.

Partnership models: Resident's Welfare Associations (RWAs) can seek to become partners in governance. Recently, the state government in Delhi has sought to marginally empower welfare associations by giving them house tax collection and assessment functions, the power to impose fines, and the authority to monitor municipal work such as desilting of water tanks, cabling, road widening, the maintenance of parks and parking places, and the distribution of water tankers. This is a step in the right direction, but perhaps a small step. Welfare associations should seek to have a greater share of the pie. However, their involvement in governance will be effective only if they display an ability for such responsibility.

Too often, welfare associations are riddled with infighting; they turn a blind eye to encroachment on public land by influential members of the association; they take no action against the pilferage of electricity by their own members; and the office-bearers monopolize the services that the association is supposed to provide to all the members. If RWAs continue to be of this nature, there is little hope for them or their members.

Role models: It's important that we meet people who have fought the system successfully. Such folks are living proof that there is merit in having the courage of one's convictions. Their success is a reminder that although the odds may be against us in taking on the establishment, perseverance and principle pay. It would be a useful idea to have such people speak in Rotary Clubs, Lions Clubs or service and residents Associations.

Consumer Protection Act: The Consumer Protection Act came into existence in 1986. It is a comprehensive piece of legislation, giving Indian consumers the right of redressal against shoddy goods and sub-standard services. However, according to one survey, it is significant that eight years after the Act, over 80 per cent of the people in the country are totally ignorant about its existence. Even those who are aware of the law know nothing about how to benefit from it. This is a sad commentary on the educated in India, since, after all, the Act is for the protection of citizens. Journalist-activist Pushpa Girimaji who has done an excellent book on consumer rights says this about the scope and impact of the Act:

> From the postal department and electricity boards to schools, hospitals and housing boards, no one was spared. Manufacturers and traders were mercilessly hauled up before the courts for overcharging, for under-weighing, selling sub-standard goods and for poor after-sales service. For the first time, Indian consumers began to question the quality of service rendered by professionals like lawyers, architects and doctors. Public utilities providing basic services like transport, power supply and telecommunication, which till then believed themselves to be invincible, suddenly found themselves at the receiving end.

Any piece of legislation is as good as what citizens make of it. Of course, the working of the Act has had its deficiencies. Many consumer courts have been non-functional because of vacancies. Such courts also suffer because of lack of infrastructural facilities and procedural delays. But there are also advantages. Take a look at these random examples:

- A widow whose insurance claim is arbitrarily rejected by the Life Insurance Corporation can knock at the doors of the consumer court and seek justice.

- A bank depositor can hold a bank liable for the loss of valuables kept in its locker.

- A victim of adulteration can seek compensation for the injury and suffering caused by consuming such food.

- A doctor can be asked to pay damages for the consequences of a negligent action.

It would be useful if citizen groups or RWAs circulate a copy of the Consumer Protection Act to members and keep updated records of how it functions. Consumers on their part need to follow certain elementary rules:

■ Keep proper documentary records.

■ When you buy something, always collect a receipt.

■ Demand a receipt even for services rendered.

■ Always read warranties/guarantees carefully.

■ Cash receipts often have conditions of sale printed on them. These too should be kept carefully.

■ When making a complaint, always ask for the complaint registration number and note it carefully. Once a complaint is attended to, always ask for a receipt which states the task performed, the date on which it was undertaken and the amount charged, if any.

■ Maintain a file of all agreements/deals/any other documents that you have signed.

Apart from the Consumer Protection Act, there are several other pieces of legislation which every concerned citizen should be aware of. For instance, there is the Standards of Weights and Measures Act, Prevention of Food Adulteration Act, and Drugs and Cosmetics Act. Knowing these laws does not automatically mean that you dash off to litigate. But if you are aware of the law, you are in a position to demand what is your right and this can convey to the provider of goods and services, including government agencies, that you are not willing to be taken for a ride, that you are willing to fight for what is your due.

Legal action in most cases is, quite rightly, the last resort. Public pressure could be a more immediate and effective tool. It means the hassle of convincing others to join in. Perhaps many cups of tea and many heartfelt discussions. That takes time. But it costs a lot less money than going to court. And it's for *you*, isn't it?

As always, many of the above suggestions are indicative. If you've been thinking on these lines already, you may have even better notions on how to fight injustice. Our idea is simply to emphasize that there are both civic and civil ways to fight wrongdoing, and a person who adopts any or all of the above remedies is less likely to feel suckered or shortchanged and more like a social winner. Of course, the task is daunting. But think about it. What if the person asking for a bribe knows that:

- You will not pay?

■   Not only will you not pay, but if your work
    is not done, you will write a letter to the
    press, or to your MP or MLA, or to the
    corrupt creature's boss?

■   Moreover, you are willing to take a
    delegation of your residents' association or
    other vociferous groups to visit the offender
    next day to demand an explanation?

Is it not entirely likely that this officer's habit
of being high-handed and corrupt will receive a
fairly unusual jolt?

We can't say it often enough, that the most
important step is to *make* the resolve not to be a
mute witness to wrongdoing to yourself, or, ideally,
even to others. Of course, to implement this resolve
we need to 'take *amrit*', in the Sikh sense, that we
ourselves will not compromise. We, alas, are the
subverters of our own system. And, in the end, we
end up being its victims. Therefore, it is extremely
important that the search for justice begins by
turning the searchlight inwards on ourselves so
that *we* can make the resolve to be honest and
above board.

One thing is certain. If everyone becomes a

colluder in an unjust set-up, the system will collapse.
There are strong signals that this may already be
happening. In 1995, as many as 180 out of the 425-
member Uttar Pradesh Legislative Assembly had
criminal records, and among those who contested
elections in Bihar there were as many as 243
candidates who had cases against them in court.
The Uttar Pradesh government in 1998 had a
shocking 19 ministers with criminal records,
including one with 37 murder indictments pending
in court!

So, if the system collapses, with it will collapse
our dreams and expectations. Therefore, it is only
our own *enlightened long-term self-interest* which
can compel us to be *citizens* in pursuit of a just and
civil social order and to be sufficiently above board
ourselves to stand up against public wrongdoing. It
is equally important to remember that those who
fight for a cause larger than themselves feel a
sense of exhilaration and satisfaction, of being
vindicated, which is a reward unto itself. They
become a role model, a symbol of hope for others,
and a convincing proof for themselves that it is
desirable and indeed possible to take a stand, and
win.

4

NGOs: Support Strategies

It really boils down to this: That all life is interrelated. We are caught in an inescapable network of mutuality, tied to a single garment of destiny. Whatever effects one directly, affects all indirectly.

—Martin Luther King Jr.

If we accept that it is imperative to move from being educated and relatively privileged Indians to being Indian *citizens*, a question arises: is there an alternative forum, outside the government, where we can actually contribute as citizens?

For too long, any such thought has been stifled by the sterile belief that it is either the government or 'somebody or something else' who will take the lead in such an endeavour. The so-called Indian citizen has fallen flat between these two stools.

There is little doubt that in the India of the new millennium, its citizens will need to involve themselves more actively and constructively with the process of nation-building outside merely those avenues provided by the government. Indeed, the growth of such a 'non-governmental sector', with a far greater voluntary participation of the country's citizens, must itself become a conscious policy of the government.

Over the last five decades, the non-governmental sector has grown in India. It is an emerging network, as yet rather fragile and in many areas less than noticeable, and certainly mostly penurious.

It appears to be also characterized by a multiplicity of efforts, still largely on the margins, lacking a coordinating centre, dependent mostly on charities, and not without its charlatans. And yet, for its inadequacies, there does exist an NGO network in India to which the concerned citizen can turn should he or she be so inclined. There are several important aspects of this network to note.

■   First, a large number of such organizations

are involved in crucial areas such as poverty alleviation, skill enhancement, primary education and health care upgradation. Many of them deal with the empowerment and inclusion of women and disadvantaged children.

- Second, the NGO network exists almost across the length and breadth of India. You have only to look around: some NGOs, usually in the greatest need of support, both financial and moral, exist very close to where you stay.

- Thirdly, the manner in which you can become involved has a great degree of flexibility. That is precisely the definition of voluntary involvement. Thus, your involvement can be in the nature of financial help, and that is a commendable policy instrument! Such donations are also eligible for tax exemption under Section 80 {G} of the Income Tax Act. If you wish to do more, your involvement can be through part-time donation of service, the *shram daan* or *kar seva* strongly urged by our own social and spiritual traditions.

- Fourthly, it is not necessary that such an involvement should be at the cost of what is your primary involvement, be it a business, profession, service, home-making, child-rearing or any other duty/vocation. Voluntary assistance to NGOs is an extra, over and above your mainstream occupation. But the good news is that you can work it into your routine without jeopardizing your bread and butter or your daily commitments.

- Fifthly, voluntary donations of the non-financial kind are a valuable area of involvement. Most NGOs need medicines, books, blankets, utensils and any other surplus items that often languish unproductively in a regular middle-class home.

- Sixthly, such a pursuit needs to be conscious but also cautious. There's a lot of doubt across the middle-class spectrum about the bona fides of non-governmental organizations. There is nothing wrong in having such doubts. Voluntary action cannot be enforced. It cannot be legislated into law. That would be a contradiction. Instead, we must be convinced when we associate with an organization that its credibility is beyond doubt, and that it's not a scam, a front with an altruistic label simply to collect funds. It is perfectly in order, therefore, to check out the actual working of a particular NGO and verify its goals and delivery systems.

How can one check out whether an NGO really does what it claims to do? This is not such a difficult matter to resolve. A little effort is all that is required.

- You could drop in at the office of an NGO unannounced.

- You can visit by appointment and ask the right questions.

- You can ask to see its published brochure, or go beyond that to see the annual report.

- You can ask questions about the budget and how much is spent purely on administrative purposes. The higher the administrative costs in proportion to development investment, the warier you need to be. You

could tactfully ask what solid good its
members have achieved by flying around to
seminars (if they have, that is!). How many
ideas have they been able to actualize as a
result of such exposure and networking?
The last is an important question, but often
it also presupposes a certain attitude
towards NGOs.

It is important to point our here that the
cynicism about NGOs that we encounter so often
can be both unfair and unintelligent. The truth is,
an NGO also needs to have efficient administrative
systems to run it. We need to overcome the diffused
notion in our minds that NGOs are ragtag
organizations which should somehow always run
on a shoestring budget, as 'selfless' organizations
who spend nothing on themselves and work
'emaciatedly' for the good of the people. This is a
false notion. NGOs work for the good of the people,
but to be successful, they need to be run efficiently,
with a well-managed and effective administrative
system and a capable, decently paid staff to ensure
optimum delivery and the best utilization of funds.
We must, therefore, allow NGOs to use a certain
percentage of their funds for administrative

purposes without jumping to the conclusion that we're dealing with an organization which seeks only to feather its own nest.

For instance, if an NGO runs a school, it needs money not just for the building, if it has one, but also to pay the teachers. Better pay attracts better teachers, and most of us accept this in the case of public schools, but when dealing with special schools run by NGOs, the same logic does not apply. We expect these institutions to survive on the bare minimum; teachers in these schools should do their job on a purely voluntary basis, out of the goodness of their hearts.

To our minds, one of the most poignant examples of this is to be seen in schools for disabled children. We were horrified to discover that in a couple of such schools in Delhi, the parents of some truly unlucky children refused to countenance even a modest hike in school fees. In a gruesome echo of the discrimination against the girl child, such parents reserved their best resources for their 'normal' children and grudged spending on a handicapped child, threatening to keep her or him wholly at home instead, without any stimulus from the outside world.

We're certainly not barbaric ancient Spartans

who exposed their newborns overnight, outdoors, to cull the fittest. But if we thus *punish* our helpless and our frail, or the institutions that look after them, we lose our honour.

So, while it makes sense to convince ourselves that the NGO we wish to support is genuine, we need also to re-examine our own attitudes and educate ourselves.

The most efficient way to verify an NGO is to see its operation in the field. Deprivation is so painfully visible in India. The poor are not difficult to find. And it is equally easy to see the impact of an organization which *has* made a difference in the quality of such deprived lives. For instance, the beneficiaries of an NGO working in skill enhancement should be helping people to not only make better products, but also earn more money. (Perhaps they're good at one and not the other? Maybe *you* could help in marketing.)

Similarly, those in the ambit of an NGO which is seeking to empower women will look and sound more confident, they will have learnt to identify and articulate their problems, and they'll have a ground plan for betterment. An NGO which claims to be working for slum children can be judged by a single visit to its city or field centre. Are its loos clean? Are the walls bright with children's efforts? Don't look for perfection: you could probably help make their centre better equipped. Instead, sniff the air for *attitude*—the NGO may have recently begun work and not impacted much yet, but it may be bursting with sincerity and lovely ideas. If you like the sound of the people in it, that's your best guide as a first deciding factor.

You could help make their ideas happen, but remember: don't try to take over or bully the founders, because they need support, not interference, to accomplish their work. However, if you do smell a rat in the way they function, *and have proof*, either disengage or tip off their sponsors. Remember, if you have ego hassles with the founders, you may score off, but the beneficiaries will suffer neglect.

It is actually very difficult for any NGO to camouflage either its good points or bad. What we need is to step out of our routine existence and check out the actual working of organizations which interest us.

Indeed, there are many examples of successful NGOs that are role models for those who wish to create organizations of their own. Once again, the incentive to do so is the fact that there is a dramatic need for more people outside the government to work in such areas as poverty alleviation, primary education, women's empowerment and primary health care. These are of course the most obvious areas where a new NGO can begin to make a difference if properly organized. However, there are other areas where you can make a difference to both the quality of life of others and your own well-being. A random example is garbage. All our cities are more dirty than they should be. Delhi alone has 1,500 tonnes of garbage which is not removed every day. Our markets are filthy. Our back-lanes are dirty. Our garbage dumps are factories of disease. Our gutters overflow with sewage. If, for instance, you make the resolve to collect like-minded people to establish a society or an organization to tackle the efficient removal of garbage even in your own area, it is already a valuable instance of public-spirited work. Other areas of work are equally important: sanitation, hygiene, the maintenance of public parks, consciousness of environment, pollution control, the propagation of family planning. These are just indicative areas.

The most important thing is our conviction that well-intentioned citizens outside the government can carve out areas of socially relevant work and effectively achieve desired results.

It is not difficult to organize an NGO of your own. The first step is the awareness within you of the need to do so. Everything else will come about. As Gandhiji said, Find a purpose: the means will follow.

The second thing is to identify an area of work. This could be anything of importance around you. It is not necessary to completely negate your self-interest in this venture. For instance, it could be an area of environment, such as the maintenance of a public park, which is important for you as well as for those around. It could simply be the making of a small cement ramp between the steps and removing turnstile gates to give your park wheelchair access, or planting and maintaining a few trees.

A word of caution to ourselves here. Don't let's waste too much time on evaluating the eventual impact of our efforts. In fact, the biggest mistake is to measure cause and effect in overly proportionate terms. If we do, our effort will appear to be so negligible that we won't even want to begin. A spot of *nishkaama yoga* (action without getting desperate about the result) works very well indeed as a long-term rationale.

It's even more important that we should get *started*. If hundreds and thousands of us are similarly motivated, gradually the very face of India will begin to change.

So how do you set up an NGO? It is not difficult to set up an organization of your own in support of a cause which you believe to be important. Here's how you could go about it:

Identifying a cause: This is the first step. It should be a cause which agitates you. It should be a cause which you believe in. It should be a cause which you have taken the trouble to study thoroughly, including examples of similar work done by others in the area.

Motivating people: A cause requires the participation of citizens. You can be the prime mover but you need to involve others. Some causes are very easy to sell, specially if they pertain to the immediate self-interest of others around you. Some are more remote in their impact, such as the removal of illiteracy or the empowerment of women in the underprivileged areas, and require greater skills of persuasion.

Establishing goals: Many causes flounder because

of undefined goals, or goals which are too ambitious. It is useful to make small beginnings with clear-cut objectives which can be feasibly implemented. Later, one can build upon these.

Registering a society: The following steps need to be taken in order to get a society registered:

File the following documents with the registrar of societies:

- Covering letter requesting the registration of the society.

- Memorandum of Association in duplicate along with a certified copy.

- Rules & regulations/By-laws in duplicate, duly signed.

- Affidavit on non-judicial stamp paper stating the relationship between the members, duly attested.

- Documentary proof regarding premises shown as the registered office of the society along with proof of residence of all the subscribers.

- On formation of the society, apply to Director
  (Exemption), Income Tax Department, for
  registration u/s 12A, on Form 10(A).

- Apply on Form 10(G) to Director
  (Exemption), Income Tax Department, for
  claiming exemption u/s 80G.

- Registered societies with specified objectives
  can further apply to the Income Tax
  authorities for claiming exemption u/s 10[21]
  to 10 [23C] of the Income Tax Act.

These steps may appear difficult, but if you
consult a lawyer specializing in such matters, you
will find that he or she will quickly put together
the entire documentation.

Raising Funds: This can be a difficult task because
people in India often want the desired results but
will not open their wallets to support a cause. But
this is not an insurmountable obstacle. Once people
realize the long-term benefits of collective action,
they are willing to contribute.

Initially, it is useful if the amounts from
individual contributions are small. As the
organization grows, and its effectiveness is

established, such contributions can increase.

It is also useful to raise funds through *corporate sponsorships*. If a cause is good, there is no problem in openly seeking financial support for its implementation. Many NGOs are hesitant about doing this. They also lack a clear-cut fund-raising strategy. They do not know how to approach funding agencies or individuals or corporate houses for money. They do not know how to organize fund-raising events such as a concert, a fete or a sale. These are operational handicaps which must be overcome.

There is enough money floating around in our cities. And, with effective persuasion, a considerable amount can be collected for good causes.

Some funding support is also available with the government. The Ministry of Social Justice & Empowerment has a system to empanel NGOs for financial assistance. Other government departments have their own schemes. It is always useful to explore this possibility. In fact, the government should consider ways and means to encourage the creation of NGOs, and increase the quantum of assistance that can be provided to them, while simultaneously improving the system of monitoring their effectiveness.

In fact, we believe that NGOs can both supplement and complement government initiatives. They cannot replace governments, nor should they. Once formed they have to be careful not to adopt solely donor-driven agendas, or play the role only of well-heeled consultants, ignoring their empowerment and advocacy roles. It is also necessary to be vigilant about some NGOs which become corrupt, absorbing donor funds while being cavalier in the delivery of services. Yet, the essential and vital role that NGOs play in a civil society is of transforming individuals into concerned human beings; of reducing the dependency of citizens on the state; and, indeed, of widening the experience and exposure of residents in a manner that they become citizens, capable of acting outside the apparatus of the state for the general well-being of society. It is for this reason that we believe NGOs need to be provided the right incentives by government and access to financing where feasible along with such government support which can make more effective their quality of service for the poor and the underprivileged.

Contrary to some of our beliefs, it is not as if we have inadequate experience in setting up voluntary organizations outside the government. Urban India, in particular, is dotted with voluntary groupings such as residents' associations, service groupings, Rotary Clubs, Lions Clubs and so forth. These are useful forums, bringing together people of a certain neighbourhood or profession or those with identical views. Many of these associations are involved in issues larger than their own interests. However, it is also true to say that most of them have restricted themselves to being a lobbying forum for only those causes which are in their immediate interest. Of course, this too is a valid pursuit. But there is a great scope for many such associations to dramatically widen their area of work so as to encompass issues of wider public concern.

Such associations can also help in the formation of NGOs, either under their own auspices or even as a resource service to help other citizens in doing so. The Lions and the Rotary Clubs can play a particularly useful role in this regard.

Finally, the most important reason for your involvement in an NGO, or your efforts to create one, *is yourself*. It is our experience that those so involved lead far more satisfied lives. They live in the routine world, but are more efficient in coping with it. Their extensive involvement gives them a wider view on life and a greater scope for personal fulfilment. These are individuals who know that in however small a way, their effort *can* make a difference. What's more, they can actually see this difference unfolding around them.

Beyond the predictable contours of the daily grind, which indeed is the lot of most of the middle class, these people have an area of escape which is simultaneously a contribution to society. All our religions teach us the virtues of compassion and of returning to society what we have taken from it. This kind of involvement makes that religious conviction possible. Of course beyond religion, it is, once again, personal interest that above all dictates the need for this involvement. Either we must help to change things, or things will so deteriorate that they will destroy hopes of our own security and prosperity.

5

Squirrels at Setu

While the Vanara Sena toiled to build the bridge to Lanka, Rama walked amongst them, enthusing his army with his heroic presence. Suddenly a small flurry caught his eye. It was a little grey squirrel, straining to lift the biggest pebbles it could in its tiny paws. It carried each pebble carefully to chinks between the large boulders hurled down by the Vanaras. Back and forth it ran industriously, intent on its task, nimbly dodging heavy feet, flying splinters of rock and the sudden splash of inquisitive waves tossed up by the Ocean.

Rama watched it silently awhile and quietly beckoned to Lakshmana and Hanuman. Becoming aware of their glance, the squirrel stopped, abashed. 'What do you do here, Little One?' asked

Rama gently. 'I saw You had begun a mighty
work, Lord', faltered the squirrel, 'I wanted to do
my share'.

Rama held out his hand to the valiant little
creature and with one jump the squirrel nestled
trustingly on his palm. Tenderly, the Prince of
Ayodhya stroked his benefactor's soft back. 'Thank
you, dear Friend. I am fortunate indeed to have
you on my side.'

—The Ramayana

Are you alone in lamenting the state of our
nation? Surely not! Early on, it grabs us all. If
we're teenagers we feel the pinch of poor public
transport, the lack of decent bus shelters, good
libraries, inexpensive yet smart options in eating,
dressing, living. Multiply by the power of three if
we're young adults or twenty-somethings trying to
crack the cruel code of the urban jungle. Take to
the power of ten if we're householders or senior
citizens living on retirement benefits with dwindling
socio-emotional back-up.

We tear these problems threadbare with our
intimates, we share moments of communal despair
in queues, trains, buses. Yet we tend to keep moving
if we see an accident, a drunk lying in a drain, a

dead cow or dog on the road, or a dangerously open manhole. And what about making our pavements, parks, crossings and buildings more disabled-friendly or elder-accessible?

Where do we begin, we may ask. Who will listen? What can one conscience-stricken but helpless individual do?

But people like us have indeed managed to begin doing things that have shown definite results quite soon. Like us, they too felt the need for positive social action. And they went ahead to do something about it. Their small but precious initiatives contributed to big things. At first their efforts were like the pebbles carried so valiantly and sincerely by the squirrel in the *Ramayana* to help in the *setu bandhanam* or bridge-building. By and by the pebbles added and arched into entire bridges.

The examples we bring you here are merely indicative. They comprise instances actually known to us, mostly in and around Delhi. Many more such initiatives in all parts of India, we know, are still unsung. They wait to be discovered by you, to have you strengthen them. Meanwhile, here are some modern Indian squirrel stories.

Mobile Creches

In 1969, the year of the Gandhi Centenary, Meera Mahadevan, a housewife and writer, was appointed to a women and children's sub-committee to observe the centenary year. She noticed that while construction workers toiled to build the Centenary pavilion in New Delhi, their children lay on rubble in the dust and heat. Meera's simple response was to provide the children with shelter. These children, as we all know too well, lack nutrition, health care, education and social skills. Their parents, usually illiterate rural migrants, are themselves too disadvantaged to rear them properly.

Today, thirty years later, Mobile Creches, the organization begun by that one Delhi housewife, has 23 centres in Delhi, Mumbai and Pune. Ten are in the capital itself. There are day care creches for infants (0-3 years), now extended to play-schools (*balwadis*) for toddlers (3-6 years) and NFE (non-formal education) for children between 6 and 12.

Mothers start lining up to deposit their children at the creche between eight-thirty and nine every morning. The babies go through a well-planned day: meals, naps, play time, health check-ups, a daily dose of vitamins.

Their older siblings in the adjoining *balwadis* are also kept busy through a day of exercise and lessons while the NFE children are taught basic maths, science and Hindi. At 4 pm the mothers come back from the day's work to fetch their children.

Meera operates from Gole Market, New Delhi ('Mobile Creche', DIZ Area, Raja Bazaar, Sector IV). To contact her, call 336-3271, 334-7635 or fax her at 334-7281.

People vs. Pollution

We're sure you've seen those Maruti vans around Delhi whose paintwork proclaims them to be mobile pollution-checking units. Did you know they are driven by the initiative of two young Delhi businessmen, Satya Sheel and Saurabh? Brothers and comrades in a shared fight against pollution, they were appalled to discover that 7,500 people die every year in Delhi of respiratory diseases caused by vehicular pollution—Delhi has more vehicles than Mumbai, Calcutta and Chennai put together.

Rather than wait for state action, the brothers

set out in early 1997 to mobilize schoolchildren
against pollution. They were stunned by the
response from the first 15 schools they approached.
By the year's end they had enrolled 220 schools
and three lakh children. That summer, one lakh
children monitored the pollution levels of at least
five vehicles each around home. Those who
monitored the most number of vehicles were given
certificates endorsed by celebrities and by the
transport department that had by now joined the
cause. Tulika, the brothers' organization, also
rewarded the two most active students with a free
nature camp holiday in the Himalayan foothills.

An on-the-spot painting competition against
pollution drew 17,000 school participants for which
business houses donated paper (Ballarpur), drawing
boards and crayons (Maruti), free snacks and tents
(Maurya Sheraton), free drinks of Milo (Nestle),
free biscuits (Bakeman's) and free gift hampers
(Minto).

The mobile pollution-checking vans are also the
combined result of corporate donations. All this
took literally two years to achieve. But more than
the idea, it was the persistence of Satya Sheel and
Saurabh that delivered such helpful results to
Delhi's choking citizens.

To get in touch with Satya Sheel, write to him at Tulika Public Service Division, PO Box 101, New Delhi-110 001. You could also call him at 625-6700 or fax at 625-3115.

Deepalaya

'Nothing is for free,' That's one of the slogans of Deepalaya, 'The Abode of Light', an organization meant to provide primary education to Delhi's poor children in 40 slums and two railway stations. Its pupils pay a very nominal sum as school fees so that they have a genuine stake in society, so that they are partners with Deepalaya in changing their environment. For Deepalaya's focus now goes beyond primary education to community development, income enhancement, skill development and health care.

Yet its first pupil was a *dhobi*'s son in 1979, when Deepalaya was created by T.K. Mathew of Venmony village, Alapuzha district, Kerala. Mathew had migrated to Delhi in 1962 and led a comfortable middle-class life. But he wanted to repay his social debt. He himself had been educated only because a few public-spirited citizens had put up a shed and started a school through voluntary contributions.

So along with six friends who were fellow churchgoers, he began Deepalaya with five children, two teachers and an investment of Rs 20,000 contributed by the seven founding members. Twenty years later, Deepalaya tends to over 20,000 slum children on a budget of around three crore rupees. But Mathew says Indians somehow prefer donating for the construction of houses of worship rather than for the education of a poor child. Deepalaya has only 1,600 sponsors yet. This is a shame, considering that it takes only Rs 2,000 a year to sponsor a slum child's education.

Deepalaya's address is 46, Institutional Area, D-Block, Janak Puri, New Delhi-110 058. Their telephone numbers are 554-8263, 559-0347 and 559-0348. The fax number is 554-0546.

Common Cause

In 1980, H.D. Shourie was 68 years old, retired from an averagely successful life as a bureaucrat. But instead of fading away into the sunset like he could well have, he plunged into voluntary public action. He founded Common Cause. It was a nonpolitical, non-profit, voluntary organization. Anyone could become a member. Its aim was to seek redress for people's problems, through the free services of concerned people. Routine costs would be met by a nominal subscription charge.

One of Common Cause's first cases was to do with pensioners not getting their dues. Shourie wrote to the editor of a leading national daily, asking aggrieved pensioners to send him letters addressed to the prime minister (then Mrs Gandhi). He got 9,000 letters. When he asked to meet Mrs Gandhi, to hand them over, he was delegated to an official. So he piled 9,000 letters in to the boot of his car and drove off to South Block. But nothing happened. So Shourie filed a writ petition in the Supreme Court. A public-spirited lawyer had agreed to fight the case, free! A year later, the petitioners won. This landmark decision by the apex court benefited four million pensioners.

This first case established the bona fides of Common Cause. Thereafter, this organization has helped establish consumer courts in every Indian district. It has activated the improved functioning of blood banks, intervened in cases where rights were affected by the levying of property tax by Delhi's Municipal corporation, improved the efficiency of various public sector services like electricity, telephones, banks, airlines and so on. Public accountability is its greatest goal. It has even won its petition to the Supreme Court that the expenses of a political party in a constituency should be clubbed with the expenses of the candidate. And it's thanks to Common Cause that political parties are pressured by law to file annual income tax returns.

Exhausting work? Sure, but H.D. Shourie does not look like a feeble octogenarian. There's a spring in his step and a twinkle in his eye. Common cause now has 5,000 members including several social luminaries. Shourie receives 30 letters a day which he replies to, aided only by a steno and a messenger. His telephone rings constantly. He's just moved office from his dining table to premises bestowed by Vikram Lal, Chairman and MD of Eicher Good Earth and a member of Common Cause's Governing Council.

The Chief Khalsa Diwan

The Chief Khalsa Diwan, with its headquarters in Amritsar, is a 100-year-old organization. The members of the Delhi chapter are prosperous, successful people. But they weave *seva* into their day's work, the service to humanity which is Sikhism's strongest tenet.

Health is a priority of Sikh community work. Accordingly the Diwan has set up the Guru Nanak Medical Centre in the compound of a gurudwara at Nehru Nagar, off the Ring Road at Srinivaspuri.

A core fund donated by ophthalmologist Dr Manmohan Singh funds the free treatment of the poor and needy in neighbourhood slums. Patients register for a mere five rupees and get free medicine besides voluntary clinics from senior doctors. And donations keep coming. People give both money and medicines.

The Diwan has ventured even further. It has dug a free borewell that gives clean drinking water round the clock to nearby slum dwellers. Fourteen thousand people were treated in 1997-98 and many more saved from sickness by the availability of clean water. Plus, the Diwan has adopted Khichripur village near Ghaziabad and is teaching local women tailoring skills and has also set up a thirty-two-room home for the old and infirm in Rajendra Nagar.

What motivates the good Sikhs of the Chief

Khalsa Diwan? *Apna Tapta Paropkar*—exactly like
the Gurus ordained. Service through sacrifice—
sacrifice of time, money, effort and attention.

Jailhouse Rock

Arun Kapoor is very much a city man. He is the
principal of a prestigious school in Delhi. He lives
in a nice home, drives a good car, has the occasional
drink, enjoys parties and being with his family. But
five days a week, after school, he's in Tihar Jail,
working with the young inmates of Jail No 5. There
are as many as 1600 prisoners there between the
ages of 16 and 21.

Initially Arun was asked if he could organize
some books for the young people. He went to
personally deliver them and found himself agreeing
to set up a library in a room promised by the Jail
Superintendent, Dr A.K. Shringla. Today the library
has 5,000 books of which as many as 100 are issued
daily. Hind Pocket Books has donated many. More,
the inmates are taught library skills. An essay
competition is held every month and those who
can't read and write are voluntarily taught by
those who can. Best of all, this opening up of the

world of books has made the youngsters receptive
to the vital counselling they need to get back safely
into society when their time comes.

Streetkids' Cop

Amod Kanth grew up in the small towns of Bihar.
His father was a scrupulously honest official who
suffered for it. His nickname was 'Bihar's Gandhian
Magistrate'. Amod went to teach in Jamshedpur
after college. Within a year he left his institution,
a well-known one, to start a college for tribals and
factory workers in the Jamshedpur-Chaibasa belt.
It ran into major management problems. Amod
then sat for the Civil Services Exam and joined the
Indian Police Service in 1974.

Posted to Delhi, Amod accompanied the Lt
Governor of Delhi, H.L. Kapur, to the huge slum of
Jehangirpuri. He noticed there were at least 25,000
street children in that one area. Impulsively, he
asked the Lt Governor for two small flats from the
Delhi Government to set up a work centre, even
offering to pay rent. And so Prayas (Effort) was
born in 1987, initially as a contact programme,
helped by volunteers from the Delhi School of Social
Work.

Today Prayas is involved in the care of over 2,500 street children in Delhi. It has 27 centres of non-formal education, 15 centres of vocational training and an involvement in 14 public libraries for street children. The children also benefit from the Prayas Health Service, a hospital and a 15-bed nursing home. Children get at least one set of clothes for summer, a sweater for winter and a pair of shoes each. Action Shoes has donated at least 1,000 pairs. Prayas employs more than 150 people and has an annual budget of one crore rupees. It owns property worth several crores. Of the 10,000 children who have been through Prayas, 6,000 earn a living today.

But Amod says there are miles to go yet. At least half a million children roam the streets of our capital. Of these, as many as 70,000 don't even have shelter. A lone police officer is doing his bit. Many more of us can pitch in, with not much 'prayas' on our part.

Get in touch with Amod by phone—331-9742, 335-2678. Or write to him at Prayas, JCP, Police HQ, ITO, New Delhi.

Bagh Bahadur

When TV personality Vinod Dua shifted house to
Old Delhi, he was dismayed to see that the historic
park of Qudsia Bagh was near dereliction. At the
housewarming party held by Vijay Kapoor, the Lt.
Governor of Delhi, in his official residence, Vinod
expressed his concern. Vijay Kapoor promptly agreed
to do something about the park that held pleasant
personal memories of college days. He inducted
Vinod as the chairman of the action committee, a
rare case of a non-bureaucrat in such a post.

The committee began investigations in right
earnest and was shocked by the incursions of a
private restaurant, a self-styled imam illegally
occupying a Mughal mosque protected by the
Archaeological Survey of India (complete with water,
electricity and telephone connections), and a tennis
court semi-permanently serving as a marriage
pandal. On the basis of the committee's interim
report, this vandalism is now being rectified, despite
the presence of strong vested interests.

Love and Longing

When Shyama Chona's daughter Tamanna was

born with cerebral palsy, she wrenched herself beyond her mother-grief and made herself see the baby as a message from God to do something for disabled children. She and her army officer husband did not have money. Given his transferable job, she worked as a UGC lecturer in several cities around India. For nine years, Tamanna could not even raise her neck, but lay passive in her mother's lap while Mrs Chona corrected papers or read. A round of hospitals abroad offered zero hope of recovery. But Mrs Chona learnt a lot about how to cope. Inspired by Tamanna's own name, which means longing, Mrs Chona registered the eponymous organization in 1984. Donations came miraculously when an article on her was published.

Today Tamanna's outreach program seeks to help disabled children in Punjab, Delhi and Haryana, with 200 such on its daily rolls. Few people understand the long, slow, daily trial faced by the parents and families of disabled children. 'It's like falling into a dark pit,' says Mrs Chona, who is also the powerful principal of Delhi Public School, R.K. Puram. 'You keep climbing out of it, but suddenly you slide back inside. And then you must climb again'.

Perhaps it is her profound recognition of the

cyclical nature of grief that allows this mother to keep going. For even sorrow needs its honourable due, only after which it can transmute into the will for action. If you can help, contact Mrs Chona, Tamanna Special School, D-6, Vasant Vihar, New Delhi-110 057.

Kids for Elders

HelpAge India was created in 1978 to do something for senior citizens, who today number 70 million. (We ourselves may figure in the expected 2025 count of 177 million). The joint family system has broken down significantly, there's less space in urban homes, a greater demand on family income, and a general tightening of life that leaves the elderly very vulnerable and lonely. And 90 per cent of our elders come from the unorganized sector, which means no pension, provident fund or medical insurance when they turn 60.

HelpAge's aim is to fund-raise for voluntary agencies that care for the elderly. In its first year, all it managed was a meagre 22 lakh to fund 13 projects. In 1998 it raised 13 crore and helped fund 500 such organizations! HelpAge India takes no

money from the government. The biggest chunk of
its money—rupees four crore—comes from donations
by schoolchildren. Not elite schools either, but
humble government schools. Direct mail appeals
fetch about two crore. Only one per cent of the total
funds come from HelpAge greeting cards.

HelpAge is directly involved in two activities:
arranging cataract operations for the old (in 1998 it
did 57,000) and mobile medicare units for the
destitute aged. There are eight such units in Delhi
alone and 95 all over India.

The HelpAge activity we love best is their Adopt
A Gran scheme. You, as a family or as an individual,
can sponsor an elderly person. Their daily needs
will be met through monthly contributions of Rs
400. HelpAge sends you 'your' Granny's or Grandpa's
picture and, if you like, you can meet them and be
involved in their rehabilitation. It's such a shame
that only 28,000 people in all of India have
responded to this scheme. Could it be that we only
value those who are functional and productive?
Our treatment of the disabled says so. But age is
the one master disability that will grab each of us
one day. It is investing for our own sunset years, if
we care for our elderly now.

More than the money even, it is emotional involvement that is worth investing. Like those kids in government schools whose parents are teaching them profound values by donating for the old, despite their own limited incomes. You can call HelpAge in Delhi at 011-6852916/6865675 or write them at C-14, Qutub Institutional Area, New Delhi 110 016.

Mom for MedAlert

Nirmala Bhushan is an average middle-class person. She lives in a middle-class housing colony. She and her husband both held salaried jobs in a state government office. Her son is a computer consultant in the US. She took voluntary retirement in 1990. Par for the course so far.

Well, in 1997, when this good lady went to the States, she read an article in the *Reader's Digest* that sent her into a tailspin. Almost as soon as she landed home, she got cracking on doing something in India about the idea that had fired her so: Medical Alert, a system of metal-tagging people with their blood group, essential information about conditions like diabetes/asthma/heart valve implants and a phone number for Medical Alert India which is monitored 24 hours and can instantly retrieve full information from its records about any member for the hospital or the police.

Such services are useful not only to accident victims but to those with communication disabilities. Mrs Bhushan has spent Rs 30,000 out of her own pocket and her son sends her money from abroad to help her project.

So far only 20 people have enrolled with Medical Alert India. Her relatives chide her about her obsession, but Mrs Bhushan says, 'I have received so much from society, I want to give something useful back.' If you'd like to help her, why not call her at 011-2726040/2721782? Or write to her at Medical Alert India, 14, Kallol Apartments, 35 IP Extension, Patparganj, New Delhi 110 092.

Doc Against Drugs and AIDS

Dr R.M. Kalra is currently Professor and Head of Educational Measurements and Evaluation in the National Centre for Educational Research and Training (NCERT). He acquired his degrees in USA and Canada and worked with American and

Canadian pharmaceutical industries. He happened
to sit next to Mother Teresa in December 1992 on
a flight home from Dhaka, after a UNESCO
assignment in Bangladesh. This encounter
strengthened his resolve to do something for society.
He began to research drug addiction and AIDS,
searching out Delhi's addict enclaves. This field
work led him to focus on addiction among Delhi's
young. His findings came out as a book, *Drug
Addiction in Delhi's Schools*. This book has been of
great help to educationists. He is now engaged in
yet another useful public service, mapping the
changing profile of drug addiction. If you want to
tap his expertise to set up work in your neck of the
woods, just call Dr Kalra at 011-6220596.

Harmala of Hope

Cancer is likely to grow as a giant killer in India.
It almost finished off Harmala Singh, daughter of
the famous soldier General Harbaksh Singh and
wife of JNU professor Deepankar Gupta. But
Harmala survived and looked for means to help
other cancer patients. She was joined by newsreader
Jitender Tuli, himself a cancer survivor. Calling

themselves Cancer Sahyog, they began work under
the aegis of the Indian Cancer Society. Just by
going up to the OPD in the Breast Clinic at AIIMS
in Delhi and telling people, 'We are survivors', they
brought hope into many lives. Emotional support
groups were set up, soon spreading to three other
medical centres.

But Harmala soon realized that 80 per cent of
cancer patients in India are at the terminal stage.
They and their families need not just courage to
face the situation but also 'palliative' care, to help
them live the last of their lives with dignity and
comfort. So Harmala formed another non-profit
society called Cansupport, specializing in palliative
care. Its concrete activities are to provide
information to afflicted families, professional
services from doctors and nurses, emotional support,
and, whenever possible, the care and support of
needy children with cancer. There's a lot of
ignorance about cancer. Even educated people think
it's contagious.

Harmala needs a lot of help: volunteers and
mobile teams of doctors, nurses and counsellors—
at least four such teams in a large city. She also
wants to open a Poor Patients' Fund. The annual
membership for Cansupport is Rs 500. Life

membership is Rs 2,500. Donations are tax-exempt under Section 80 G of the Income Tax Act. You can contact Harmala at 1, Palam Marg (Annexe), Vasant Vihar, or at 011-6145515/6115815. Her private number is 011-652823, on Mondays, Wednesdays and Fridays, between 12 noon and 2.00 pm. You could do this kind of work in your town or neighbourhood and Harmala will be happy to share her knowhow on the practicalities.

Iqbal's Cleaning Brigade

One of the most noticeable features of India after Independence has been the increasing acceptance of filth in our lives—and here we are speaking of actual filth, as in garbage and trash. As we have said before, in Delhi alone, about 15,000 tonnes of garbage goes uncollected every day. We may be obsessed with personal cleanliness, but we are quite comfortable with collective filth. We try and keep our own houses clean but ignore the garbage just outside. We have a bath every day but will do nothing about the refuse lying unpicked in our backyards.

The situation is fast reaching crisis proportions.

That is why what Dr Iqbal Mallick is doing is so important. Iqbal moved to the Asian Games Village in 1991. It was a quiet and green area, but dirty. Every day, with her eight-year-old son in tow, she would go to throw the garbage from her house at a collection depot. She wanted to put the garbage into the dump, but the place was so dirty and slimy, and emitted such a foul smell, that she would, like the other residents, just throw it somewhere near the dump.

Like the other citizens, Iqbal too could have accepted things as they were and not bothered about what was outside her home and immediate family. But she was different, and decided to tackle the problem. To begin with, she motivated the residents of the Asian Games Village to contribute a paltry sum of Rs 15 per family. With this money in hand, she contacted the local rag pickers—18 years and older. Eight of them came to work with her.

Iqbal paid the rag pickers to segregate the garbage at the dump. The biodegradable garbage was taken to an adjoining wasteland for composting. This was done scientifically, by composting the garbage below the soil, so that it did not give out any foul odour. The non-biodegradable garbage, such as glass, metal or plastic, was sent to the recycling industries. Within a few weeks, the biodegradable garbage had become manure and could be sold at two rupees a kilo. The scheme had become financially self-sufficient, and the Asian Games Village had become a cleaner locality.

Iqbal's concern as a citizen had led her to create a truly successful project. Its greatest strength was that it was a decentralized system. It did not need huge landfill sites, or expensive loaders or trucks. It needed merely tricycle rickshaws, a *phawra*, a *geti* and a *jhadoo*. It generated employment, but was inexpensive.

The success of this experiment led to it being replicated in other areas. Today, Iqbal's Cleaning Brigades (as she calls them) are working in 27 colonies, schools and colleges in Delhi. Her approach is to set up the system and when it is functional, hand it over to the residents' welfare associations or other concerned organizations.

For those who want to clean up their neighbourhood, Dr Mallick and her organization, Vatavaran, can be contacted at 649-3881.

6

What Can I Do?

When Prajapati, the All-Father, created the three races of Devas (Celestials), Danavas (Humans) and Daityas (Titans), he bade them go forth to inhabit the three worlds.

'Give us each a watchword to live by,' they begged. And He did.

'Damyata (Be restrained),' He told the Devas, who had magical powers.

'Datta (Give, be generous),' He urged the race of men, for they were interdependent for survival.

'Dayaadhvam (Be merciful),' said He to the Daityas, who were endowed with ferocious strength.

Thus when you hear the thunder roar and crash DA DA DA, it is none but our All-Father, reminding His children to be restrained, generous and merciful.

—Brhadaranyaka Upanishad

If your life is too tight or your resources too stretched to allow much by way of social engagement, there are still important contributions you can weave into your everyday life that will assuredly make a difference. Some of the small, practical ideas listed below were originally compiled for the August 1998 issue of *Zena* magazine in an article, 'The Zena Guide To Middle Class Survival', inspired by the Big Idea of *The Great Indian Middle Class*, and elicited a positive reader response.

If some of the points listed here sound like they belong in a book of handy hints, you're right, they do. To come within kissing distance of the sublime, there's a lot of the ridiculous to deal with first—the messy minutiae of life, that sound grander by far if you quote Mies Van der Rohe (part of a pre-Nazi design movement called the Bauhaus) and declare, 'God is in the details.'

Please treat this chapter as your personal idea bank. Do share your ideas with your circle of friends, your kitty group or *mahila mandal*, your golf, cricket or tennis club or your yoga, music or art class, your gym, your band, your *satsang*, or Buddhist chanting group or church group, your service officers' club or any other gathering of which you are a member.

You might even like to celebrate special birthdays, anniversaries or graduations and promotions with a request to your friends and family to make donations to a charity of your choice or sponsor a hospital bed, a child's education or plant a tree in your name.

Or your colony/neighbourhood/building association might like to collect funds for a cause when Deepavali, Id, Baisakhi or Christmas come around.

Meanwhile, we share below some specific options for action that you might like to read, consider and select from.

Education

Check this out for contemporary meaning. This is Poem No. 183, *Potuvial*, written by the ancient poet Pandian Nedunchezhiyan in the days of the Tamil Sangam. You'll find it in a famous collection of verses called the *Pura-naanooru (Four Hundred Poems On The World)*, complementing the *Aga-naanooru (Four Hundred Poems On The Heart)*:

Even among those with births from one mother,
The mother's mind changes in its attitude
   according to

The worth of the education received by them:

Even among the many born in one clan, the king
Will not choose the eldest, saying to him, 'Come',
But will follow the path of the learned one
     among them:

Even among the four social groups with known
     differences
If one belonging to the lower class is educated,
Then even the one in the higher class will
     approach him
(For learning from him, regardless of his status).

It is indeed beneficial to acquire learning,
The teacher has to be helped, if in difficult
     circumstance
And he has to be given needed wealth in good
     measure:
And there should be no aversion (on the learner's
     part)
To the state of reverence for the teacher.

If this was the importance given to learning
centuries ago, then the large number of our
countrymen who cannot read and write makes
nonsense of our claim to be civilized today. But
beyond this, and again from the prison of our own
self-interest, it is very important to remember that

estimates have proved that primary education has the highest social rate of return, followed by secondary education. According to a World Bank study, primary education was the most important component in East Asia's rapid growth in the last three decades.

So what can we do in our own little ways to help change things? Here are some ways to start making a difference:

- Donate a fixed amount of money regularly to a government school in a slum area nearby where classes are irregular or are inadequately equipped. Perhaps you and your particular group could build their roof, buy them a water cooler—and show them how it must be cleaned and maintained—plus, teach them the value of dustbins.

- Donate, donate, donate, to individuals and institutions working with disabled children. Such children are so hopelessly situated, they really have nowhere else to go. Small schools run by very committed and loving individuals, like ASTHA (Alternative Strategies For The Handicapped) or

Samadhan (Early Intervention Centre), both Delhi-based NGOs working with disabled children, are often in more dire need than the larger institutions. A timely donation to such smaller schools may literally save them from being forced to shut down. Best of all, help them find secure premises, they get pushed around a lot by landlords.

■ Finance textbooks for poor children—your maid's, washerman's or chowkidar's.

■ Sponsor a child's education. Organizations like Deepalaya, CRY, SOS Villages, Nehru Bal Samiti and the Salaam Balak Trust are well established routes to poor children.

■ Don't give away last year's textbooks to the junkman. Donate them to the nearest government school or any organization that works with street/slum children. You could probably gather a whole trunkful if you ask each house with children in your colony.

■ Want to get rid of surplus story books or comics? Set up a small library in a corporation school where English is taught. Or *buy* them a set of discounted books in the appropriate language from the next book fair you visit. You could also pass on educational games and toys.

- Adopt a primary school in a slum or village and periodically collect funds from your colony to buy them something they need.

- Alternatively, adopt a vocational training centre for underprivileged girls. You could collect funds to buy them sewing machines for their sewing class or an oven for their bakery class. If you're good at that sort of thing, you could even teach them yourself. And once they have the basics, they would always find good use for baking equipment that's not too expensive to gift: patty pans, cake tins, icing cones, ingredients. Or cloth (and designs) for the sewing class to make simple aprons, gloves, potholders and table mats. You could even rent a stall at your colony's deepavali mela and sell what the children have made, giving the proceeds to them.

- Make one adult literate. Your maid, your chowkidar, your driver. Just teach them basic words and numbers. This is the hardest task of all, but you could always get an NGO or even your children's school to suggest a teaching plan. For inspiration, or simply because it's a well-told story that we Indians can relate to, read *Inside the Haveli*, a wonderful novel by the late Rama Mehta, published as a Penguin paperback. It's the story of a Rajput daughter-in-law in Udaipur who manages to swing some interesting changes even while respecting tradition. We found this book by chance, loafing around the pavement bookstalls near Churchgate in Mumbai, and presumptuously think you'll like it, too. Curiously, it's got a hearty recommendation on the cover by John Kenneth Galbraith, of all people, the Kennedy administration's ambassador to India from long ago, who described our country as 'a functioning anarchy'.

■ Spread this true story:

The mother of a quadriplegic spastic child was tormented by people who kept on about bad karma. One day, while out wheeling her son in their lane, she was accosted by an old fakir who gazed intently at the child and declared that such children were 'bhrasht yogis'. They were highly evolved souls who had missed moksha by a whisker and were compelled to take one more birth as human beings. They chose to be born handicapped, so that they would be incapable of either wrong words or wrong deeds. All they knew was how to give and receive love. To raise such children was maha punya, the greatest possible merit, said the fakir before he disappeared.

Isn't this positive, parent-friendly interpretation a better rationale than 'bad karma'? It may even bring about a change in the attitude of our society towards the disabled, specially the hopelessly disabled. We need so much to include the 19 million Indians who suffer from one or another handicap. People with cerebral palsy alone number as many as the entire population of the state of Haryana.

The simple medical fact, as detailed by doctors in the West, is that every pregnancy has a three per cent chance of going wrong. It is merely the impersonal law of averages. Or you could suffer some shattering impairment because of war or an accident or even, God forbid, violence. *The point you can help propagate is that there is no shame or disgrace in having a disability.* For society as a whole needs to acknowledge and include people who, for whatever reason, can't get about as freely as nature's original blueprint meant them to.

Which is why we ask you to simply share the philosophy contained in this little incident far and wide: who can tell where you will plant a seed of comfort or a resolve to do something tangible? In their time, the Buddha and Jesus and, later, the Sufis, won over so many human hearts just through their parables and stories.

Changing mindsets is thus a crucial part of spreading education, though it is long, slow work. In this case, the practical benefits can be so many:

a) Architects will automatically plan buildings (including cinemas!) with disabled-access: ramps and special gates, special toilets, handrails and lifts.

b) Town planners will think of disabled-access when they put in pavements, parks (with easy gates and ramps), or plan shopping malls, zoos, stadia, housing colonies and city complexes.

c) Municipal authorities or development authorities may be motivated to fix existing complexes and buildings which are currently out of reach for the disabled.

d) Corporates may be induced to take up disability access as a worthwhile project.

Cleaning Up Town

We all agree that dirt and disorder are two of the biggest blots on the Indian landscape. But have we ever considered that chucking a sweet wrapper, an empty packet of chips, a soft drink tetrapak or plastic wraps out of a car, bus or rickshaw, are *unpatriotic* acts? Here's a list of possibilities that you might like to explore. Some of the ideas given below will cost money, others will cost time, and yet others may demand a tithe of both.

We hasten to clarify, yet again, that these are points of departure. It's entirely up to you: the 108 sanskaras that you already need to fulfil in your daily life; your inclination to do something for your self in terms of the social environment you live in. Good things can happen only by our collective will, but it's the first step taken by an individual—

you!—that can become another Dharma Chakra Parivartana (That Which Set in Motion the Wheel of Law).

- Persuade people, beginning with your family, to throw garbage in the right place. This could mean forcing your toddler—or teenager—to throw his toffee wrapper in the bin at airports, railway stations and waiting rooms. Or getting up and walking around to find a dustbin instead of stubbing out your cigarette underfoot, no matter where.

- While travelling, even if it's just to work or to drop your child to school and back, keep a junk bag in your vehicle for wrappers, orange peel, banana skins, used tissue and tetrapaks. Don't regard the road or highway as a stretch of no man's land which you are entitled to use as your private dustbin!

- If garbage in your area is not cleared like clockwork every day, do harass the municipal authorities promptly. Start pleasantly and get increasingly firm without losing your temper in round one itself. By call three, the residents' association should be in on the effort and the next person in the civic hierarchy should be notified. In fact it makes sense to react promptly, so that the authorities too feel that they are dealing with a concerned and alert citizenry.

- If you want the municipal authorities to clear away the garbage dump in your area more frequently, why not get the residents' association to bear the cost of the extra trips?

- Alert the municipality (read 'harass') if it's a rubbish heap en route to your office or a dump near your office building itself. *The whole town is your town*. You must be able to move anywhere in it with safety and hygiene.

- Take a tip from radio jockey Shamshir Rai Luthra who regularly urges listeners to call the municipal authorities whenever they spot a dead dog or cow on the road. Such carcasses are huge sources of infection and disease if left lying around for long, as they often are.

- Another tip from an entertainer: Daler Mehndi, current king of Punjabi pop, has embarked on a Green Delhi drive which includes planting saplings and installing dustbins all over the city. Couldn't you do it for your colony, or if, fortunately, you already live in a tidy neighbourhood, couldn't you try greening and cleaning an urban slum?

- Yet another cue from Punjab: remember the beautiful notion they had at Anandpur Sahib during the Khalsa tercentenary, of giving away neem, ber and guava saplings as prasad? Devotees took them home carefully to plant, either in their own gardens, or in colony parks if they lived in flats. Why not organize this at your local temple, gurudwara, church or mosque? It could be an annual event, a monthly event, or even fortnightly, with devotees signing on to sponsor, for one year, a certain number of saplings every *pradosha*. (For those who'd like to know, this is the *trayodashi* or thirteenth day of every *shukla paksha* or bright fortnight of the moon, when Shiva is supposed to dance the *ananda tandava* for all the assembled celestials. *Pradosha* always attracts huge crowds because it is such a meaningful concept: it is Nataraja's Dance of Joy that is supposed to keep Creation going.)

- Involve neighbourhood children in a fortnightly clean up drive. Why not have a treasure hunt or ecology quiz along with it, and a chocolate cake as an inducement? The children will have the added benefit of having done something worthwhile that they can talk about in school and perhaps write about as their project for SUPW (Socially Useful Productive Work).

- Persuade your company to sponsor dustbins for your city or town. It's more valuable by far and certainly more 'upmarket' than sponsoring fashion shows. Emblazoned with your company's name and logo, the bins can also carry the advertising message 'XYZ Cares For Coimbatore' or whatever. Just think of the huge subliminal points your company wins in the public consciousness at every corner and the goodwill generated because your company is seen as socially and ecologically proactive!

■ Minimize your use of plastic bags by keeping a huge jute shopper or jhola or woven basket permanently in the boot of your car. Or if you use public transport and stop to shop on your way home in the evening markets, why not carry one of those nice 'slim bags' that are convenient to fold and tuck into your handbag or briefcase? We were horribly embarrassed to discover that in Delhi alone, garbage dumps in lower-income localities have 96 per cent biodegradable matter, whereas garbage from more affluent neighbourhoods has only 40 per cent biodegradable refuse. A typical middle-class colony of 1,000 homes can generate an average of 5,200 plastic bags a *day* as refuse—shuddering heights!

■ Refuse pleasantly to accept plastic bags from the shopkeeper, or if that's impossible, ask him to give you fewer bags. Explain why you'd rather not: because it is non-biodegradable and will just add to the planet's permanent litter. There's no way to get rid of plastic: you can neither burn it (without severely polluting the air) nor will it decompose when buried in a landfill.

- Wait a minute: what do we throw the kitchen rubbish *away* in, every day, if we ban plastic bags? Don't we in fact carefully hoard and sort plastic bags by size for their million-and-one uses in daily life? Why must anything useful or pleasant always be 'wrong'? What could be a substitute for this amazingly convenient thing? We really scratched our heads over this one and here are some possibilities:

a) Just use *fewer* plastic bags very consciously instead of a total boycott.

b) Check out the local bazaar for bags made of natural fibre: one Delhi option is at those shops where ropes, cot strings and ladders are made and sold. They have closely woven jute sacks in various sizes. We could use those for dry waste. We could collect peelings, leftovers, the flotsam and jetsam from used plates (like curry leaves, spices and chillies) in a box or an aluminium tin with a lid that we can empty when the sweeper comes by in the morning. The tin is simply washed and reused. Once a week, shine it up by a wipe with a lemon peel or a rub with squeezed-out tamarind and a pinch of salt.

c) Throw the garbage direct into the bin and get the bin washed and dried every day or on alternate days, as a matter of routine.

d) If daily cleaning of the bin is impractical because you go out to work and your servant will not do the needful, why not line the bin heavily with newspapers? The problem with throwing rubbish straight in the bin arises only in the case of wet waste, bones or peelings. Newspapers will absorb the mess, if the mess is not too wet. The papers can then be bunched around the rubbish, lifted and thrown.

e) For very wet rubbish, like a pot of dal that's gone bad in the fridge, just empty it into the soil of a large potted plant and lightly turn up some soil to cover it. This makes good compost.

f) Similarly, used tea leaves are better disposed of if you knock them into a bowl or a dabba kept aside all day just for them. In the

morning, after your wake-up cuppa, empty
the lot either into a flower pot (rose plants
are supposed to like tea!) or into a special
'compost pot' allotted for that very purpose.
Just dump the tealeaf container in the sink
then for the maid to wash every morning.

g) Make a compost heap in the neighbourhood
park, with the permission of the authorities
concerned, of course. Each family in the
colony should dump its organic waste in
there and get free manure for their plants
round the year.

■ Always try to separate polythene from the
rest of the garbage and give it to ragpickers
only.

■ Encourage the local shopkeepers' association
to gather funds to have the marketplace
swept and picked clean daily. Tell them
not to dump peel, paper or slops just outside
their shops. Why not suggest that each shop
or stall invest in a huge, lidded bin?

■ 'Adopt' a public urinal and hire someone to
clean it at least twice a day.

■ Raise money to finance mobile toilets or Sulabh Shauchalayas for slums. This involves two things: fund-raising and maintenance thereafter. Maintenance involves spreading awareness of the need for shared responsibility by the users in keeping their toilets user-friendly.

These measures may seem a big hassle at first, like any new habit or endeavour always is. But once begun, it becomes as routine as brushing your teeth. And cleaning up your home is where you begin cleaning up your town, because what you send out of your house gets carted away somewhere outside.

Reducing Pollution, Saving Resources

Clear the air! Cleanse the sky!

—T.S. Eliot,
Murder in the Cathedral

■ Try to reduce your dependence on generators. Their horrible sound causes serious noise pollution while the fumes of diesel they emit give even passers-by a headache. Just imagine the plight of people stationed near them and the noise levels in your neighbourhood. It is nicer by far to invest in a really powerful invertor. They come in such neat boxes these days. And not only are they silent to run, they don't need anything but distilled water in the batteries twice or thrice a month.

- Drive less. Make a sincere attempt to join or form a car pool or cab pool. Vehicles owned by the middle class or patronized by them are the largest cause of pollution in metropolitan India. Delhi tots up the highest number of automobiles, more than Calcutta, Chennai and Mumbai put together.

- Sit down and map out the most convenient route for all those in your colony or building who travel to work in the same direction. Instead of each driving his/her own car, collectively hire a bus or mini van. Accommodate each other's office timings wherever possible. For instance, if you start or finish half an hour ahead of several others, engage yourself in something interesting in that extra time, rather than forfeit the bus home. You could surf the Net, rediscover the art of writing letters, catch up on shopping, meet a co-worker or a friend in a neighbouring office for a quick chai and chat, *walk*, browse for books on the pavement or simply wrap up pending office work and feel virtuous, while earning brownie points with the boss. It's actually a win-win situation, whichever way you look at it . . . And by the way (Gosh, how did we get into this list?), you're helping the cause of the environment and saving money!

- Encouraged by the residents' associaton, a group of housewives or teenagers can visit each home with a car or a two-wheeler in the neighbourhood to see if they've got a pollution-checked certificate. The group can do something constructive for those who haven't—set up a pollution check on Sunday morning in the neighbourhood itself, with the help of the traffic police, and make sure everyone *knows* about it, by circular or small handwritten notes. This could become a regular neighbourhood activity. Keep the pressure up on defaulters, but in a way that makes them see the value of this proposition, rather than bruising their egos to the point of obstinacy. Remember, they may have sincerely meant to, but gotten careless or forgetful through sheer work pressure or ill-health or some personal problem that led them to neglect their duty as a citizen. This, in fact, is the biggest danger when we embark on do-gooding: the sin of self-righteousness, a lamentable trait that makes us very unappealing indeed to others.

■ This one's tough: let's try to work with as few lights, fans and air-conditioners as possible, to slow down coal consumption in thermal power stations. Or delay starting the desert cooler or air-conditioner by an hour every day. If lots of us do this, it's that much electricity saved. We know, we know, you're wondering why you alone should make this sacrifice when so many rich and powerful people are misusing their wealth or privilege. Let's not cynically shrug our shoulders or harangue such folks in a tiresome 'Have vs. Have Not' way (do *we* like being guilt-tripped by beggars?).

■   Instead, why not start and sustain a friendly letter and poster campaign on the benefits of reduced power consumption, for Their Affluences—wittily worded, with a gentle barb or two: provoke interest first, to be noticed. The rich are truly different, they live in extremely insulated worlds. But that does not mean they are necessarily lacking in heart, conscience or intelligence—after all, there's some terrific philanthrophic and charitable work being done by rich people. And at the end of the day, they feel as full of angst, as proud or emotional about India and Indianness as we, the Middle Class, so provenly the backbone and bulwark of Bharat Inc. As Kargil established, there are some things we *all* take very personally, whether we're Anand Mahindra or a life convict in Yerwada or a little bride in rural Orissa. The point is, why not give as much for cyclone-ravaged Orrisa's rehabilitation as for our soldiers? And why not give as much for everyday troubles that are less dramatic but as pitiful?

■ Another point worth remembering here: many rich people in their late thirties and early forties or above, actually hail from simple middle-class families. They have prospered by their own luck, merit and hard work. They are trying hard to balance their old values with their new affluence, specially in the raising of their children. They cannot fail to be receptive to what they already know deep in their hearts, if only it is activated in a positive way. So hit those corporate corridors, those small but prosperous private firms, with your letters and posters. Invite them to share ideas on saving national resources with your group, to teach you new tricks from what they have observed in the larger world outside on business or holiday travels abroad. Or at least join a brain-storming session on the subject. Just *try* asking nicely. Chances are, most people, though genuinely busy, may be tremendously pleased and touched. They're so afraid to open their mouths otherwise for fear of being thought show-offs. As Shah Rukh Khan's song goes, *Phir Bhi Dil Hai Hindustani*: when we're not being unspeakably awful, we're essentially a sentimental, affectionate people. All we need is to give the green-eyed monster a break and *appreciate* each other.

■ Dare we say this: *Give up loud, noisy firecrackers on Deepavali*?
Hold it, *please* don't slam this book shut in a temper, muttering many rude things. Sixty schools in Delhi (yes, consumerist, flashy Delhi) were part of the No Fireworks campaign in 1999 and the air in our capital was at a record level of low pollution compared to all previous (monitored) Deepavalis. The suspended particulate matter that fouls up our lungs at festival time was nice and low, comparatively, as was the noise pollution level. Look, it's all about making choices. You may choose to compromise and buy only sparklers, fountains and *chakras*, while renouncing bombs, rockets and crackers. What the abstaining (middle class!) Delhi homes did was to make their houses look festive with lots of diyas and floral arches, *torans* and garlands. Some wrote cheques for charity,

some took clothes, games, toys and sweets
to orphanages. Some bought new clothes for
an entire poor family of their acquaintance.
Some pledged to finance a poor child's
education.

The children of these housholds were only
too keen and glad to give. They did not feel
cheated of 'fun' by saying No to firecrackers.
In fact, it were the parents who took some
convincing. But this is indeed the true spirit
of any festival that celebrates the triumph
of Good. Ask His Holiness, the
Shankaracharya of Kanchipuram. He's not
your average holy man. He believes that
practical, humane caring is the true work of
faith. Accordingly he started an NGO called
Jan Kalyan that works nationally, from
Tehri-Garhwal to Madhuban in Orissa, to
every district of Tamil Nadu, be it a
Sankaradeva Netralaya for the blind, a home
for mentally challenged children, a hospital,
a school or a clinic. 'Nowhere does our
religion say that you must spend lavishly to
celebrate Deepavali', he emphasizes;
'Deepavali is a time of *giving* to the poorest
of the poor. The *brightest* Deepavali is in

their eyes!' And, we may add, the healthiest, in our lungs!

Other Care

Here are some ideas on how we could make a crucial difference to our own well-being. Some of these thoughts may seem irritatingly politically correct. Many of us never troubled our heads over such issues as children, why must we now?

The answer to that is a German word, *zeitgeist*. It means 'The Spirit of the Age'. The spirit was starkly different earlier in world history. A hundred years ago the crowds in England flocked in ghoulish glee to watch public hangings. Fifty-two years ago, we Indians did not have Article 19, we did not have a Constitution that guaranteed our basic freedoms. But today? Why does the world condemn the Taliban? Why are we ashamed and horrified to the core of our beings by the Staines murder? Why do our eyes burn and our throats constrict when we remember (can we ever *forget*?) the anti-Sikh riots of 1984? Or the rapes, killings, murders, arson, looting and caste/communal conflicts that our papers burst with? Because such behaviour, considered normal in other, more violent times or places, is not acceptable in a post-War world, in Independent India, to our self-image *now* as civilized people with a human rationale for existence.

It's been a slow evolution, a layering of ideas, an accumulation of deeds, a deep ripple across the centuries—from the French Revolution, to Victorian thinkers, to reformers like Raja Ram Mohun Roy and Ishwar Chandra Vidya Sagar; from Marx and the Russian Revolution, to the Holocaust (six million killed), to Mahatma Gandhi, to Partition, which was the world's greatest human displacement (ten million), to the Democratic Socialist Republic of India. The Republic is 50 years old now in AD 2000, bathed in blood, but still clutching brave ideas in her wounded palm. Perhaps part of her *zidd* (Hindustani for obstinacy) is the champagne of self-discovery, as we learn more about ourselves with every decade. For many of us, the biggest fizz is in the discovery that quite a few old ideas, lost in antiquity, offer astonishing continuity with the *zeitgeist* today.

This self-image is in tune with the global spirit of freedom, democracy and humanitarian values. However, we all know that these concepts are regularly abused, even by the West, which mooted them in modern times. Many European countries are little better than a police state, where every move you make is monitored. Neighbours will thump on your wall if you play music too loudly. If you come home late, you can't bathe or even pull the flush in some buildings in Belgium, France and Germany, because the sound may disturb neighbours.

If Westerners go to one extreme, it seems we dig our heels in at another. We play loud religious or film music in *pandals* well beyond the curfew hour of eleven at night. We never stop to think that sick people, elders, babies, harassed and tired housewives or professionals need their sleep. We throw clumps of hair, slops, paper and peel from our balconies and windows onto the street or compound below.

Our road manners are awful. We talk loudly below homes where people are sleeping when taking leave of our hosts after a party. We honk happily even in hospital zones, zoom through stop signs, block the left lane when we're headed straight so that those behind us who want to turn left are forced to wait till the green signal. We constantly overtake from the left or change lanes without warning.

It's not a good enough excuse to say, 'Everyone's doing it, why not me?' We can at least take responsibility for ourselves, can't we? If one person does it, others will begin to follow suit. The true test is at night, with a seemingly deserted traffic signal. It's a matter of seconds to speed through it. But you never know, a truck may swing in out of the blue, or a hapless two-wheeler or cycle, whose right of way it is. And then it's too late for repentance.

For starters, here's a Good Citizen's Conscience List of things we could easily begin doing:

■   Pay taxes. Only two per cent of urban India pays taxes, so where's the government going to get money from for infrastructure and development?

■   Don't drive indifferently past accidents. Rush the victims to hospital. Remember that 82 per cent of accident fatalities can be averted if there's medical aid in the first hour itself. And it's no hassle for you, beyond this task: according to a recent court order, the police won't insist on your name and identity if you don't wish to disclose details.

- Or else, rush a victim to a private doctor. They cannot refuse to treat accident victims. A Supreme Court order unequivocally states: 'If a victim is taken to a private doctor, it is obligatory for the doctor to provide medical aid.'

- Instead of handing a rupee to beggars at traffic lights or making your local religious house fat, rich and happy, why not slip it into the donation boxes of CRY?

- Be a proud blood donor. Check out the hospitals near you and donate blood twice a year. This will help reduce dependence on professional donors who are often poor and unhealthy. Besides, every time you donate blood, you ensure its supply for yourself in an emergency. Carry your donor's card in your wallet at all times.
  Find out about blood donation camps and volunteer your services. Or get the HR people in your office to organize a regular blood donation camp.

- Count the number of kids in a chosen slum and organize a glass of milk per head every

day. You could even fund their monthly
supply of calcium and vitamins.

- Organize primary health care in a nearby
  slum through your residents' association.

- Likewise, organize immunization and
  inoculation camps for street kids or nearby
  villagers.

- A family planning centre for women is a
  great project to organize and sustain. There
  has to be a kindly gynaecologist and a
  capable, sincere nurse, plus a cleaning
  woman and a person to keep records. Get
  volunteer services for the last task. It could
  even be you and your friends, taking turns
  for a few hours each week. This centre could
  advise on contraception and refer women to
  liaising hospitals.

- A centre like this could also organize the
  distribution of free condoms.

- Check out health care centres near you for
  what they lack. A compounder? Equipment?
  Chairs and tables? Fans? Stationery?
  Medicines and vaccines? A cleaning woman

to maintain the premises? A coat of cheerful, bright paint? A play area outside, with a minder, to allow the mothers a chance to see the doctor properly?

■ Adopt a village, but that doesn't mean you have to fix everything that's wrong with it in one go. Prioritize the needs. You might like to begin with having a tubewell bored. Or even a handpump. Just think, 80 per cent of our people do not have access to clean drinking water. If that includes you, in your apartment, harass the municipality (see chapter on Sarkari Vows). But if you and your friends go a little beyond, to that one village, you create a ripple that ultimately comes back to you.

7

My Citizen's Checklist

Use this as your personal agenda card to instil in yourself the painful new habit of bothering to do something. We suggest you make photocopies of these page to fill in every month. Keep this list pinned to your office soft board or under the fridge magnet. Maybe each person in the family/office team would like to put up one, so it becomes like a game, a game with a serious underlying purpose.

It is important to take stock periodically of everything you've managed to do. This list is a small starting point. You probably have better ideas yourself! Do share them.

Here is the checklist—

Passing by:

- Have I called about removing an animal carcass from the road?

- Have I called about removal of garbage from the road/debris from a pavement/ open manhole?

- Have I thrown things out of the window of a vehicle today?

- Do I always carry a junk bag for drives and journeys?

- Do I observe traffic rules meticulously, no matter how angry or tempted?

- Do I let pedestrians cross?

- Do I allow cyclists more than a sporting chance to make it safely?

- Do I slow down through puddles to avoid splashing others?

- Have I spat paan on the road? (It's a nauseating sight for others. I could use a spittoon or a junk bag).

- Have I chased after and scolded road hogs

who block left turns or overtake from the left?

- When parking, have I blocked access-exit for other vehicles?

- Have I parked neatly, to economize space and allow room for others?

- Have I preferred to *walk* a few yards, rather than block the road by selfish parking?

- When the lights fail, do I let others go first?

- Have I jumped queues at airports, stations, cinema halls, shops, banks? In fact, have I *forced* others to queue along with me? It's easy to do!

At home:

- Did I throw hair, paper, cigarette butts, etc, out of the window?

- Did I empty kitchen slops/ dustbins in open public territory? (Have I trained my servants to throw garbage neatly and *only* in the appointed bin, not outside or around it?)

- Do I pay residents' association dues religiously?

- Do I grudge any extra payment for amenities? It is as much for me as for the others, after all.

- If seepage in my house is affecting the neighbour, have I found the time and money to rectify it fast?

- Do I play my TV or music too loud? Neighbours could be ill/studying/ in need of peace and quiet.

- If I'm planning a dance party, can I convince others that it's possible to have a good time without blasting the music?

- If my kids play gully cricket, have I asked them to move down to open ground?

In the neighbourhood:

- If there's a Devi *jagran* night on, do I ensure the loudspeakers are not too loud and that the music stops at eleven sharp, like the law says?

- Do I block public roads or grounds for private ceremonies without checking to see if neighbours' vehicles can come and go freely?

- Do I call the municipality/tell my residents' association if there's garbage lying around?

- Do I attend residents' association meetings regularly?

- Am I involved in at least one neighbourhood betterment project?

- Do I check on the underprivileged areas around where I live? What is the state of primary health care? Are children inoculated? Do people have access to basic guidelines on hygiene?

- Do I donate something regularly to the servants' children in my locality?

As a citizen:

- Do I get my vehicle pollution-checked regularly?

- Do I call and report buses/factories/*bhattis*/ industrial plants that emit foul smoke?

- Do I donate a percentage of my salary every month to a good cause? Am I increasing that amount periodically?

- Have I volunteered at least two hours a month in public service—either reading to the blind, or working with the disabled, etc? Am I increasing this time gradually?

- Have I thought of donating unused but usable medicines to an orphanage or destitute home?

- Have I seen what surplus clothes I can easily donate to the needy?

- Have I considered spending a few hours every month to make at least one person functionally literate?

- Am I involved with at least one NGO in a meaningful way?

PS: We wanted to compile a masterlist of NGOs for you, but that would need a whole book to itself! Instead, here's a website address where you can get the low down and pick according to your area and inclination: **www.indev.org.**